INVISIBLE WOUNDS

UNDERSTANDING and HEALING FROM

COMPLEX PTSD

JOHN P. BOYLE

AUTHOR OF APPALACHIAN KID

INVISIBLE WOUNDS
Understanding and Healing from Complex PTSD
© 2026 by John P. Boyle
All rights reserved. Published 2026.

DO NOT REPRODUCE WITHOUT PERMISSION

No part of this publication may be reproduced or transmitted in any form or by any means, electronic or mechanical, including photocopying, recording, or any information storage and retrieval system now known or yet to be invented, without written permission from the publisher, except in cases of brief quotations in critical articles and reviews.

The design elements of this book were produced with the help of AI.

Scripture quotations taken from the Holy Bible, New International Version®, NIV®. Copyright © 1973, 1978, 1984, 2011 by Biblica, Inc.™ Used by permission. All rights reserved worldwide. The "NIV" and "New International Version" are trademarks registered in the United States Patent and Trademark Office by Biblica, Inc.™

Published in the United States of America by

Spirit Media Publishing

Spirit Media Publishing
www.spiritmediapublishing.com

Spirit Media and our logos are trademarks of
Spirit Media Inc
205 S Academy Street #3251
Cary, NC 27519
1 (888) 800-3744

Books | Health, Fitness & Dieting | Mental Health | Post-traumatic Stress Disorder

Paperback ISBN: 979-8-89307-218-1
eBook ISBN: 979-8-89307-219-8
PDF ISBN: 979-8-89307-220-4
Library of Congress Control Number: 2026902584

Dedication

For Kyla, Jack and Anthony, whose love made every page possible.

Table of Contents

Introduction

If you're holding this book, I want to start by telling you something I wish someone would have told me a long time ago:

You're not crazy.

You're not weak.

You're not broken.

You're not failing at being a human being.

You're hurting.

And if you're hurting, I want you to know you are in the right place.

For most of my life, I had no idea I was living with Complex PTSD. I didn't know childhood trauma could follow you into adulthood like a silent shadow. I didn't know the panic, the hypervigilance, the emotional spirals, the insomnia, the perfectionism, the people-pleasing, and the fear of conflict were symptoms, not personality flaws.

All I knew was that I felt different from everyone else.

More reactive.

More anxious.

More overwhelmed.

More ashamed.

On the outside, I looked fine.

I had a great career.

I had degrees I was proud of.

I had a family I loved.

I had achievements stacked like armor.

But on the inside, I was exhausted.

I was scared.

I was confused.

And I was drowning in things I couldn't name.

This book is the book I needed back then.

I'm writing it because I don't want you to wander as long as I did. I don't want you to blame yourself for things that were never your fault. I don't want you to feel alone in symptoms that millions of people experience but rarely talk about. I don't want you to mistake survival responses for character flaws the way I did for far too many years.

If you've ever wondered:

"Why am I like this?"

"Why do I react so strongly?"

"Why can't I just get over the past?"

"Why do I shut down?"

"Why do I feel unsafe even when I am safe?"

"Why do I feel unworthy, no matter what I achieve?"

"Why doesn't anyone understand what I'm going through?"

Then this book is for you.

My goal isn't to diagnose you. My goal is to explain what is happening in a way that feels like you're finally being spoken to, not spoken about. I want to demystify trauma. I want to give language to things you may feel but have never been able to put into words. I want to show you the science behind your symptoms without overwhelming you. And I want to share my story in a way that doesn't retraumatize you but helps you recognize your own strength.

Most importantly, I want you to know this:

Healing is possible.

Hope is real.

And you deserve both.

People often ask me why I would write about something so painful.

Because pain loses power when it's spoken out loud.

Because healing grows when it's shared.

Because someone out there is where I once was, and I can't stay silent knowing they're living in the dark.

I believe God carried me through things I didn't understand so that I could turn back and help others. I believe none of us are meant to heal in isolation. And I believe your story matters more than you know.

In these pages, I'm going to take you through my journey, not to center myself but to walk alongside you as you navigate yours. We'll talk about trauma in the home, trauma in the body, trauma in relationships, trauma in success, trauma in silence, and trauma in faith. We'll talk about misdiagnosis, coping strategies, emotional spirals, and the nervous system. We'll talk about the helpers, the lifelines, the miracles, and the hope that carried me.

My prayer is that somewhere in these chapters, you will feel seen.

Somewhere in these pages, you will feel understood.

And somewhere in this book, you will begin to believe, truly believe, that healing is possible for you too.

You do not have to stay stuck in the patterns that survival created.

You do not have to walk alone.

You do not have to keep living as if danger is always around the corner.

There are other ways to live, to breathe, and to exist.

And together, we're going to walk toward it.

So take a deep breath, settle in, and let's begin.

I'm honored to walk this journey with you.

— John

PART ONE:
Naming the Invisible Enemy

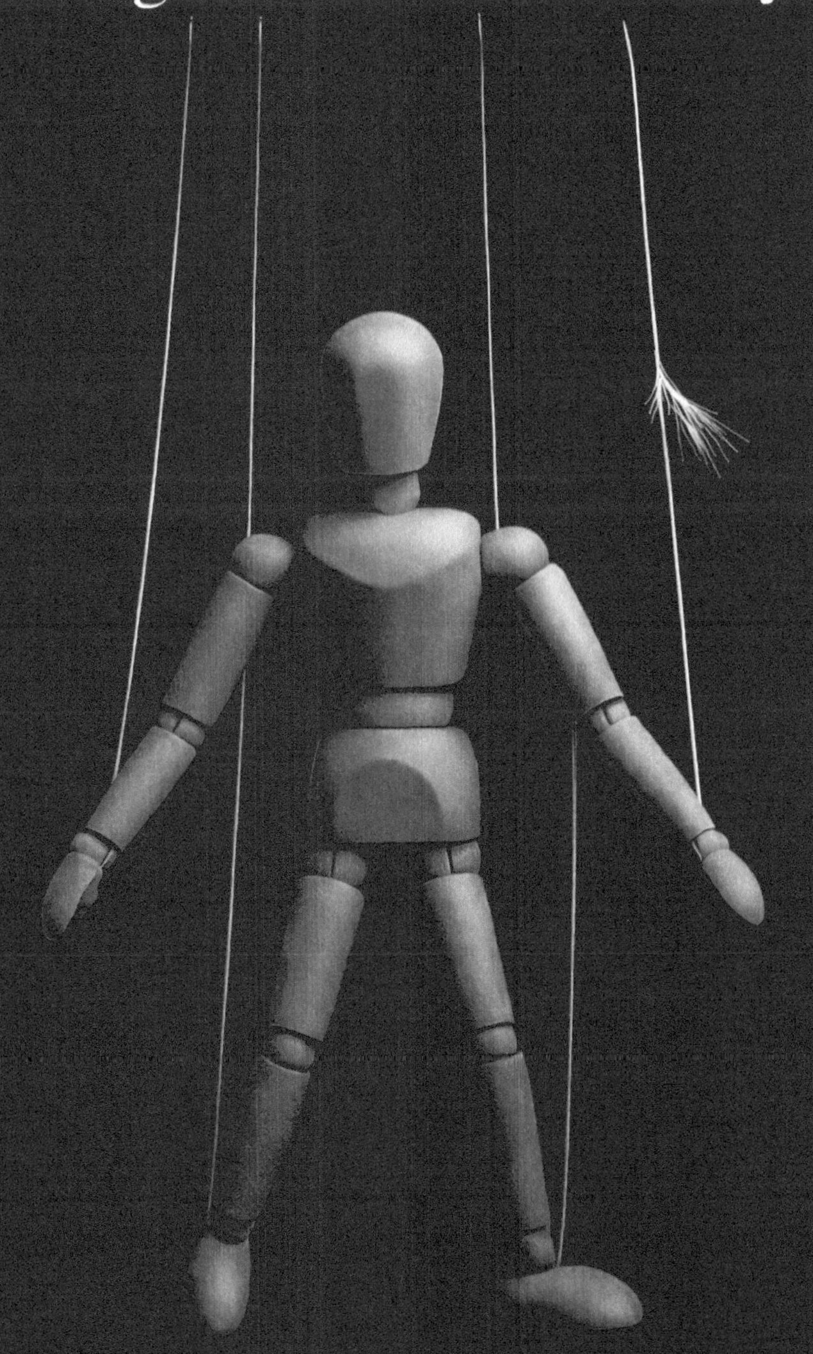

CHAPTER 1

You're Not Crazy, You're Injured

For most of my life, I believed my pain meant I was defective. The sleepless nights, the startle responses, the headaches that felt like a storm behind my eyes were things I called stress, anxiety, or bad nerves. It never occurred to me that what I was really living with were the scars of unhealed trauma.

It took nearly four decades before someone looked at me with compassion instead of confusion and said words that changed everything:

"John, you're not crazy, you're injured."

Those words cracked something open in me. For the first time, the chaos inside me made sense. I didn't have a character flaw. I had **Complex Post-Traumatic Stress Disorder.**

The Early Years: Living with the Big Bad Wolf

When I think about my childhood, the images come in flashes. They aren't full stories with clear beginnings and endings, but scattered moments. The sound of footsteps on the stairs. The way my heart would race at the creak of a door. The tension that hung in the air like static before a storm.

I grew up in the mountains of West Virginia, in a small town where everyone knew each other's business but no one really knew what went on behind closed doors. From the outside, we looked like a normal family. My father ran a successful business, my mother kept the home, and I had everything I was told I should be grateful for.

Inside those walls, though, it was a different world. There was volatility, bursts of anger that came without warning, and emotional swings that left you dizzy. As a child, I developed a sixth sense for danger. I could read my mother's breathing, her footsteps, the set of her jaw, and know when the "Big Bad Wolf," as I came to call it, was about to appear.

In *Appalachian Kid*, I once compared my family to the story of the Three Little Pigs. Each of us built our houses out of different things: denial, deflection, distraction. But the wolf always came. And when she did, I learned to go very still. That stillness became my superpower. If I didn't move, didn't speak, didn't exist too loudly, maybe the storm would pass over me.

The Day My Body Broke

At age ten, another kind of wound arrived. One morning, I was rushing to finish my breakfast when I heard the school bus turn onto our street. As I stood up and slung my backpack over my shoulders, my mother suddenly struck me in the head with such force that I collapsed onto the floor. The blows kept coming as I lay there dizzy, crying, and disoriented. In that moment, I realized they weren't going to stop. Something in me shifted. I got up, decided to defend myself for the first time, and started swinging back. For a brief second, the shock on her face made me think I might have changed the dynamic, until her expression hardened into something far worse.

I managed to block a few of her punches, and because of that her rage only grew. She outweighed me by a wide margin. With all her strength, she shoved me backward, slamming the base of my spine into a doorknob. I dropped to the linoleum floor in agony. She kept striking my head until everything went dark. When I regained consciousness, I heard her stomping through the house, screaming for my father. The moment he appeared, she pointed at me and yelled, "He hit me," again and again. Instead of protecting me or even asking what happened, my father turned to me and said I was wrong, blaming me for defending myself against her attack.

Only later did I learn that all of this happened because I had not finished some scrambled eggs.

I cried alone in my room for days, trying to make sense of what had happened. Eventually I internalized it and did my best to move forward. For years I blamed myself for the actions my mother took against me. That's what traumatized children do. We translate tragedy into guilt. If something bad happens, it must be because we caused it.

Even after my back healed, the fear stayed. My body remembered what helplessness felt like. Every muscle learned to brace for impact. I didn't know it then, but that injury became the perfect metaphor for my life. The physical pain faded, but the invisible injuries remained.

Adolescence: Building a Mask

By my teenage years, I had perfected my mask. I was the achiever, the funny one, the helpful kid. The more I could do for others, the less anyone would look too closely at me.

When the pain inside grew too loud, I buried it under performance. Scholastic achievements, sports, student leadership, anything that proved I was okay. But the truth was that I wasn't okay. I was terrified all the time.

I prayed routinely, asking God to make me different, to take away the anxiety, the nightmares, the sudden flashbacks that made me feel like I was right back in that house. My prayers didn't bring instant peace. Instead, they planted a quiet promise: You are not alone, and this is not the end of your story.

THE UNTOLD STORY OF MALE TRAUMA SURVIVORS

Men are taught to push through.
To "man up."
To handle everything alone.
To swallow tears and turn emotions into silence.
But here's the truth:
Men suffer from C-PTSD in ways society rarely talks about.
We hide symptoms behind achievements.
We bury panic under work.
We drown fear in alcohol or isolation.
We normalize rage, shutdowns, and distance.
We call survival "strength."
But silence isn't strength. It's suffocation.
Being a male survivor doesn't make you weak.
Speaking about it makes you courageous.
And healing becomes possible the moment you allow yourself to be human.

The Mirror Moment

Years later, when I volunteered at my hometown high school, I didn't expect anything spiritual to happen. I was there as a successful businessman giving back to my community. But during one small-group discussion, a mistreated teenage boy looked me dead in the eye and said, "God doesn't love everyone. He plays favorites."

Those words hit me like a lightning bolt.

I saw myself in that boy, the same hollow ache and the same quiet despair. In that moment, I realized that my success hadn't healed me; it had only distracted me. I could still see the scared child inside, begging for love he didn't think he deserved.

That was the day I stopped running from my past. I started to wonder if maybe, just maybe, God had brought me into that room to show me the reflection I'd spent years avoiding.

The Diagnosis That Saved My Life

A few years earlier, sitting across from a trauma-informed therapist, I finally learned the name of my invisible enemy. He explained that C-PTSD develops not from one traumatic event, but from chronic, inescapable stress, usually during childhood. It is what happens when the people meant to protect you are the ones who cause you pain.

As he talked, I felt both exposed and understood.

I thought about all the times doctors had labeled me with depression, anxiety, even bipolar disorder. None of them fit. But when he described C-PTSD, the hypervigilance, the emotional flashbacks, the toxic shame, the broken fight-or-flight response, the physical tension, I knew he was describing me.

For the first time, I felt compassion for myself. My reactions weren't overreactions; they were survival skills that had outlived their usefulness.

A Disorder of Reactions

I often describe C-PTSD as "a disorder of reactions." It is not about what is wrong with you; it is about what happened to you.

When I hear a door slam, my heart can still leap into my throat. My body remembers every time that sound meant danger. Even when my mind knows I am safe, my nervous system has not received the memo.

C-PTSD rewires your brain's alarm system. Instead of turning off when the threat is gone, it keeps ringing day and night. That is why people with trauma often seem jumpy, anxious, or exhausted. Our bodies are living in yesterday's emergencies.

The Apostle Paul once wrote:

"We are hard pressed on every side, but not crushed; perplexed, but not in despair." — 2 Corinthians 4:8

That verse feels like the story of trauma survivors everywhere. We have been pressed, but not crushed. Broken, but not beyond repair.

The Mask Cracks

Even after my diagnosis, I fought to maintain my mask. I had built my identity around success: Harvard graduate, business leader, provider, husband, father. However, trauma does not care about résumés.

Eventually the mask cracked. My marriage was strained, my drinking had escalated, and my health was failing. I reached the edge of myself and realized that all the achievements in the world could not heal what I refused to face.

That is when faith came rushing back in, not as doctrine, but as rescue.

God in the Ruins

When I finally stopped pretending and fell to my knees, I found that God had been there all along. Not the punishing God of my childhood imagination, but a gentle Father who whispered, "You survived what should have destroyed you. Now let Me teach you how to live."

Scripture says:

"The Lord is close to the brokenhearted and saves those who are crushed in spirit." — Psalm 34:18

For years I thought being "brokenhearted" was a flaw. Now I see it as the opening where grace enters. Healing does not erase the past; it redeems it.

Naming Is Healing

When I finally spoke the truth, "I have Complex PTSD," the shame began to lose its grip. Naming what happened did not make me weak; it made me free. Truth shines light into the corners where lies used to live.

"You will know the truth, and the truth will set you free." — John 8:32

Healing began when I stopped seeing myself as crazy and started seeing myself as injured, and therefore capable of recovery.

You Are Not Alone

If any of this sounds familiar, if you find yourself jumpy, exhausted, people-pleasing, or unable to rest, I want you to know it is not your fault. You are not "too sensitive." You are someone whose body did everything it could to survive what it should never have endured.

In the United States alone, 1 in 4 children will experience abuse or neglect at some point in their childhood. This means maltreatment affects millions of people over a lifetime, not just a rare few. Those numbers do not tell stories, but I do. I am one of them.

And maybe, in some way, so are you.

Survivor Insight: How to Start Naming Your Pain

Write what you feel, not what you think.

Do not edit. Let your heart speak before your head interrupts.

Replace self-blame with accuracy.

Instead of "I'm overreacting," try "My body is remembering."

Pray or journal using Scripture that affirms your worth.

Psalm 34:18 has carried me through many dark nights.

Say this out loud:

"I'm not crazy. I'm injured, and I'm healing."

Closing Reflection

When I look back now, I see how every piece of my story, even the painful ones, led me here. The injury I once hid became the testimony I now share. C-PTSD is real, but so is recovery. The same God who carried me through my childhood carries me still. My body may have learned fear, but my spirit has learned faith.

If you remember nothing else from this chapter, remember this:

You are not crazy. You are not weak. You are not beyond repair.

You are injured, but with time, truth, and grace, you can heal.

CHAPTER 2

When Home Is the War Zone

They say a child's first classroom is the home. If that's true, then mine was a lesson in fear.

When people picture a "war zone," they imagine tanks, explosions, and soldiers in helmets. My battlefield didn't look like that. Mine had the smell of dinner burning on the stove, the sound of heavy footsteps in the hallway, and the same sick knot in my stomach every evening around six o'clock, the moment my mother appeared upset and about to boil over.

The erupting sounds of cookware and dishes crashing were my air raid siren.

The Paradox of Safety

Most children believe that parents are protectors. That's how it's supposed to be.

But when the people who are meant to keep you safe are the same ones who hurt you, physically, emotionally, or verbally, your world splits in two.

I learned early that love could turn to rage in a single breath. One minute I was her "boy," and the next I was a target for everything that had gone wrong that day. I never knew what version of my mother would come through the door, the one who was going to show affection or the thunderstorm in human form.

My father tried to shield me in his own way. Sometimes he pushed back against her treatment of me; other times he simply looked away, trying to keep peace by pretending not to see. That is another kind of trauma, when silence becomes the family's survival strategy.

There were nights when the shouting felt like it might split the walls. I would hide in my room, counting the seconds between each crash and praying, "Please, God, make it stop."

And when it finally did, I would lie awake for hours, listening to the quiet, which somehow felt just as dangerous as the noise.

The Big Bad Wolf

When I was a kid, the story of *The Three Little* Pigs fascinated me. Each pig built a house, one of straw, one of sticks, and one of brick, to protect themselves from the Big Bad Wolf.

In my mind, the Wolf wasn't a fairy tale. She was real, and she lived in our house.

The Wolf was unpredictable. Sometimes she slept for days; sometimes she howled without warning. The only way to stay safe was to build walls, not out of bricks, but out of silence and smiles. I became a master builder.

That story became my inner language for danger. Even now, decades later, when I sense conflict brewing, I feel that same childhood instinct to grab my tools and fortify the walls. My body remembers the Wolf.

"When I am afraid, I put my trust in you." — Psalm 56:3

Faith became my secret hiding place. I whispered prayers in the dark, believing that somewhere beyond those walls, someone was listening.

How Trauma Rewires a Child's Brain

It wasn't until years later, sitting in a trauma specialist's office, that I learned my childhood home had literally changed the architecture of my brain.

Science now tells us that a child's brain is a construction site, constantly building connections based on experience. In a safe home, those connections form around love, curiosity, and exploration. In a dangerous home, the brain builds around survival.

The result is a body that lives in "fight, flight, freeze, or fawn" mode long after the threat is gone.

That is why so many survivors of childhood trauma struggle with anxiety, memory problems, hypervigilance, and emotional swings. We aren't broken; our brains were trained for war.

The Science Behind the Fear

When I hear loud voices, my brain doesn't ask, "Is this safe?" It assumes danger and floods my system with cortisol and adrenaline, stress hormones meant to help me run or fight. The problem is, there is no tiger chasing me. There is only an argument, a slammed door, or sometimes nothing at all.

Over time, living in that state wears the body down. Research shows that people who experienced chronic childhood stress have a twenty-year shorter life expectancy on average. Trauma triples the risk of heart disease and doubles the risk of cancer. It also increases the likelihood of autoimmune disorders and chronic pain.

My doctor once told me that my "back problems" and "digestive issues" were probably stress-related. He was right, but it wasn't work stress. It was the long shadow of a childhood spent bracing for impact.

When the War Zone Follows You

When I left home for boarding school, I thought I was escaping the chaos. But the war zone came with me inside my own body.

In the dorms, I couldn't sleep unless I knew who was awake and where the exits were. I startled when doors slammed. I apologized for things that weren't my fault. I gravitated toward people who felt familiar, intense, unpredictable, emotionally unavailable.

That is one of trauma's cruelest tricks. It teaches you to seek out the very dynamics that once hurt you. Chaos feels like home because peace feels foreign.

Later, at Harvard, I learned to camouflage my anxiety behind achievement. I could give a flawless presentation while my hands shook under the table. I earned respect and accolades but couldn't sustain relationships. People said I was driven. In truth, I was running from memories I didn't want to face.

"The heart of the discerning acquires knowledge, for the ears of the wise seek it out." — Proverbs 18:15

It took wisdom, and grace, to understand that the patterns repeating in my adult life were echoes of childhood fear.

Why Children Blame Themselves

One of the hardest truths I've had to face is how deeply children internalize blame.

When the people you depend on for love hurt you, your brain can't accept that the adults are unsafe. It is too terrifying. So instead, you conclude, "It must be me."

That belief becomes the seed of toxic shame.

Toxic shame whispers:

You're unlovable.

No one wants you.

You'll never be enough.

Those lies become the internal soundtrack of trauma. They follow you into adulthood, shaping every decision, every relationship, and every self-judgment.

Even as an accomplished businessman sitting in boardrooms, part of me was still that scared boy wondering what I had done wrong this time.

The Numbers Behind the Pain

The statistics are staggering, but they matter because they tell survivors one essential truth: you are not alone.

7.2 million children are involved in Child Protective Services cases every year in the United States.

91 percent of perpetrators of abuse are parents or caregivers.

Millions of adults carry these experiences — which means there are many survivors out there, even if people don't always talk openly about it

Adults who score high on the Adverse Childhood Experiences (ACE) study are 460 percent more likely to suffer from depression and 1200 percent more likely to attempt suicide.

When I first saw those numbers, I wept, not only for the children behind the data, but because it finally made sense. My reactions weren't strange. They were statistical.

Faith Amid the Fear

There were nights when I prayed with every ounce of strength I had left. I didn't ask God for miracles, only for peace. Sometimes it came, sometimes it didn't, but I never stopped believing He was there, even when I couldn't feel Him.

Now I understand that God was present in my survival, in every hiding place, every whispered prayer, every ounce of intuition that kept me alive. He wasn't absent in my pain; He was the reason I made it through.

"Even though I walk through the darkest valley, I will fear no evil, for you are with me." — Psalm 23:4

Those words became real for me long before I ever understood them.

"WHAT TO SAY" SCRIPTS

What to Say to a Doctor
"Some of my symptoms don't make sense to me, and I need help connecting them. I'd like to explore whether trauma could be playing a role. Could we look at this through a trauma-informed lens?"

What to Say to Your Partner When You're Triggered
"I'm reacting to something that feels old, not something you did. I need a moment to settle my body, and then I want to reconnect. Thank you for being patient with me."

What to Say to Your Child When You're Dysregulated
"Daddy's having big feelings right now, but I'm okay. I need a moment to calm my body so I can listen well. You didn't cause this."

What to Say When a Relationship Feels Unsafe
"I care about you, but I need conversations to stay respectful. If voices rise or insults appear, I will take space and return when we're calm."

The Cost of Growing Up Too Fast

Children from war-zone homes grow up quickly. We become the peacemakers, the caretakers, the ones who fix everything. I learned how to defuse tension before it exploded, how to comfort, negotiate, and anticipate.

People praised my maturity, but what they were really seeing was trauma dressed as responsibility.

The problem with growing up too fast is that you skip the parts where you learn how to rest, trust, and play. By adulthood, you are still that ten-year-old, just taller and busier, carrying responsibilities you were never meant to bear.

Healing has meant learning how to be human again, not a soldier, not a performer, not a peacekeeper. Just a man who survived and is learning to live.

Rebuilding the House

If trauma builds walls, healing builds doors.

Recovery began when I started dismantling the defenses I had built as a boy. Therapy, prayer, community, each became a tool. Slowly, brick by brick, I replaced fear with faith, silence with honesty, and isolation with connection.

I used to think healing meant erasing the past. Now I know it means reclaiming it. God does not waste pain. Every scar can become a doorway for grace to enter.

Survivor Insight: How to Begin Rebuilding Safety

Name what feels unsafe. Write down the people, places, and triggers that make your body tense. Awareness is the first act of self-protection.

Create one safe space. It might be a room, a chair, a prayer corner, somewhere your nervous system can learn what peace feels like.

Breathe with intention. Inhale for four counts, hold for four, exhale for six. Slowing your breath tells your body, "We're not in danger anymore."

Reframe your prayers. Instead of "God, take this pain away," try "God, teach me what this pain is trying to show me."

"He heals the brokenhearted and binds up their wounds."
— Psalm 147:3

Closing Reflection

When home is a war zone, a child learns to fight battles no one else can see.

But here is the truth I wish I could tell that frightened little boy in West Virginia:

You were never meant to be the soldier. You were the child. The war was never yours to win, but healing is.

Today, my home is quiet. I wake without dread. That is not because I forgot the past, but because I finally faced it.

The Big Bad Wolf still visits sometimes, in memories and in dreams, but she does not run my house anymore.

If you grew up in a home like mine, know this: Your story is not over. You can rebuild, brick by brick, into something stronger than fear, a life made of faith, truth, and love.

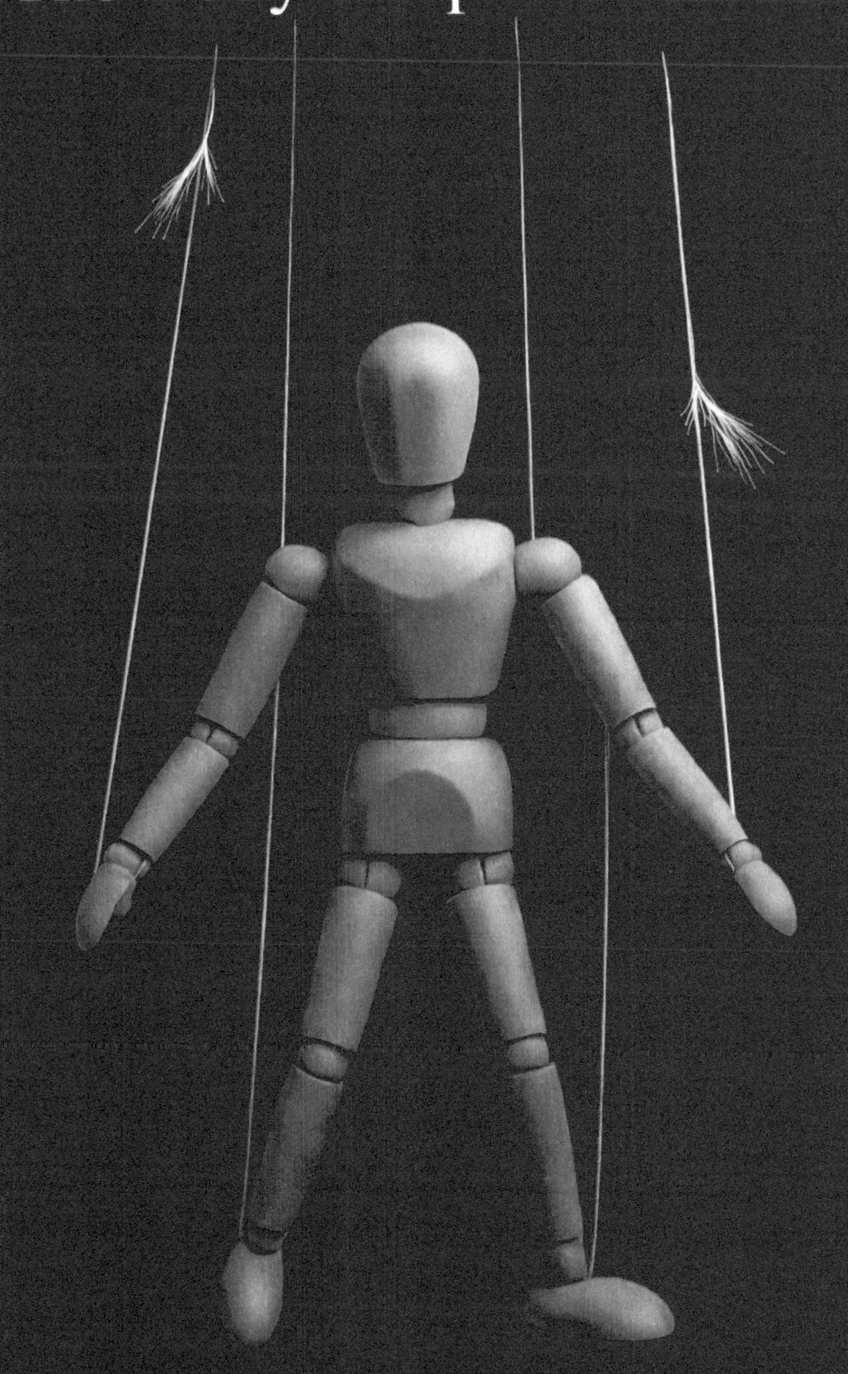

PART TWO:
The Body Keeps the Score

CHAPTER 3

The Symptoms That Steal Your Life

People often think trauma lives only in memories.

But for many of us, it lives in the body, in the muscles that will not relax, the stomach that stays tight, and the nights that stretch into dawn because rest never feels safe.

For years, I didn't connect my body's pain with my past. I thought I simply had a "bad back," or that I was one of those people who "couldn't handle stress." I didn't realize my body had been carrying a story my mind refused to tell.

The truth is, the body keeps score even when the soul wants to forget.

The Morning My Body Spoke Louder Than My Words

I was thirty-six years old when my body finally stopped cooperating.

At the time, I was running a fast-growing business, traveling constantly, and living the way trauma survivors often do, on adrenaline and ambition.

One morning, I woke up with my heart pounding so hard I thought I was having a heart attack. My chest was tight, my vision blurred, and my body trembled as if it had been running a marathon in my sleep. I ended up in the ER, hooked to machines, convinced I was dying.

After hours of tests, the doctor came in smiling. "Good news," he said. "Your heart is perfect. It's probably just stress."

He was right, but not in the way he thought. It wasn't "just stress." It was unresolved trauma that had been simmering for decades. My body had been screaming for years, and I had mistaken the alarm for noise.

The Body Remembers What the Mind Forgets

When we face danger, the amygdala, the brain's smoke detector, sounds the alarm. The adrenal glands flood the body with cortisol and adrenaline. Our hearts race, our muscles tighten, and our digestion shuts down so we can fight, flee, or freeze.

For most people, once the threat passes, the parasympathetic nervous system steps in to calm things down. But for trauma survivors, the body never gets that message. The threat may be gone, but the body keeps acting like it is still happening.

That is why so many of us live with chronic pain, digestive problems, headaches, insomnia, or fatigue. Our bodies are stuck in survival mode.

As Dr. Bessel van der Kolk writes, "The body keeps the score." I would add, "But God holds the pen." He can help rewrite the story we carry in our cells.

"Come to me, all you who are weary and burdened, and I will give you rest." — Matthew 11:28

My Body's Language Was Pain

I was ten years old when I first learned that pain could be a language. After the spinal injury that left me in pain for months, I told myself I had gotten through it. I walked again, returned to school, and went on with life.

But my body never truly forgot that helplessness. Every time I felt powerless, even decades later, the pain in my back returned. It was as if my muscles were saying, "We remember what it was like to be trapped."

Back pain, stomach problems, migraines, all became recurring visitors in my adulthood. I didn't understand then that each ache was a message: "Something inside you still needs attention."

When I began trauma therapy, my therapist explained that the body stores memory differently from the brain. The tension I carried in my shoulders wasn't "bad posture," it was armor. My insomnia wasn't "just anxiety," it was vigilance. My digestive issues weren't random, they were the gut's way of staying ready for danger.

Once I stopped trying to silence those symptoms and started listening to them, they began to soften. The body doesn't need perfection; it needs permission. Permission to stop fighting and finally rest.

SURVIVOR INSIGHT

It's Not Overreacting. It's Responding to the Past

When your nervous system learned danger as a child, your adult body responds to tiny cues as if they're emergencies.

You're not dramatic.

You're not "too sensitive."

You're reacting from a place that once kept you alive.

Trauma Changes the Rules of the Game

The hardest part isn't what happened in childhood — it's the patterns it created.

Hypervigilance.

People-pleasing.

Flinching at sudden movement.

Avoiding conflict.

These are not personality flaws.

They are survival strategies.

Your Brain Isn't Broken. It's Loyal

When your past taught your brain to stay alert, it does so long after the danger ends.

It's not malfunctioning.

It's protecting you the only way it knows how.

Healing means teaching it a new way forward.

The Emotional Thieves: Flashbacks, Shame, and Dysphoria

If physical symptoms steal your strength, emotional symptoms steal your joy.

I've heard C-PTSD explained as "a disorder of time." That's because it doesn't stay in the past. Flashbacks reintroduce the past into everyday life. Flashbacks aren't always visual; sometimes they're emotional, sudden floods of dread, sadness, or rage with no clear trigger.

I used to have what I called "gray days." Out of nowhere, I would wake up feeling worthless, anxious, or deeply sad. I would comb through my life looking for a reason and find none. Those weren't bad moods; they were emotional flashbacks. My body was reliving feelings from long ago, even when my mind couldn't remember the scenes.

Then there's toxic shame, the invisible poison trauma leaves behind.

It's not guilt. Guilt says, "I did something wrong." Shame says, "I am something wrong."

That voice of shame can be relentless. It whispered to me during every success:

"You don't deserve this."

"They'll find out who you really are."

"No one could love you if they knew."

I used to believe that voice was my conscience. Now I know it was the echo of a frightened child still trying to make sense of pain he didn't cause.

How the Brain Gets Hijacked

When the body lives in chronic fear, the prefrontal cortex, the part of the brain responsible for logic and decision-making, goes offline. The limbic system takes over.

That is why survivors often say things like, "I knew better, but I did it anyway." It isn't weakness or poor judgment; it is the brain doing what it was trained to do, survive first and think later.

Understanding this helped me forgive myself for years of "bad choices." I wasn't broken. I was hijacked. Trauma had built a reflex loop between fear and reaction, skipping reason entirely.

SEE IT

SENSORY TRIGGER

The Elevator Panic

It wasn't the height or the space that got me. It was the silence. The hum of the fluorescent light overhead. The faint rattle of the cables behind the wall. The soft ding before the doors slid shut, sealing me in.

Most people barely notice these things.

My body noticed everything.

The moment the doors closed, my chest tightened. My palms went damp. My breath shortened into shallow sips of air. The smell of metal and old carpet triggered something old, something I didn't have words for at the time. A memory without a memory.

I felt trapped, even though I wasn't.

I felt threatened, even though no one was there.

I felt the past pressing into the present.

By the time the elevator reached the next floor, my heart was pounding harder than it ever did on a treadmill. For years I told myself it was irrational, just another quirk, another overreaction. But later I learned what was really happening:

My body wasn't afraid of the elevator.

My body was afraid of being trapped.

Of being powerless.

Of being unable to escape danger.

Because that was once real.

Trauma taught my nervous system that confinement meant threat, so even a harmless elevator triggered a survival response.

The Baby Crying on the Airplane

The flight was barely underway when the baby in the row ahead of me began crying. Just a normal baby cry, sharp, sudden, high-pitched. People around me shifted, pulled out headphones, and sighed softly.

My reaction was... different.

The moment the wail hit my ears, it felt like something grabbed the inside of my chest. My shoulders tensed. My jaw locked. My heart started to thump against my ribs in a rapid, erratic rhythm. My eyes darted around the cabin searching for danger that wasn't there.

It wasn't the sound itself.

It was the helplessness.

The unpredictability.
The sharp tone that mimicked old alarms in my nervous system.
Trauma wires you to respond to distress, any distress, as if it is yours to fix or flee from.
The baby wasn't triggering annoyance.
He was triggering an ancient fear.

The Scent That Takes You Back
It was the smell that did it, a mix of stale cigarette smoke, old wood, and something sour underneath. I was standing in the hallway of a friend's apartment building when it hit me.
In a split second, I wasn't in that hallway anymore.
I was ten years old again, heart pounding, listening for footsteps.
The smell was identical to the home I grew up in on nights when tension thickened the air.
My body froze.
My breath stopped.
My mind blurred.
The hallway was safe.
My body did not believe me.
That's the cruel brilliance of trauma:
The senses remember what the mind has forgotten.

Behavioral Patterns: The Coping Strategies That Become Cages

Trauma teaches you to adapt, and those adaptations often look like success until they don't.

I became a master at reading people, anticipating moods, and smoothing over conflicts before they started. That skill made me a great leader, but it also made me exhausted.

I lived in constant hypervigilance, always scanning for threats, even in a work setting or church pews. If someone's tone shifted, my stomach tightened. If a door closed too hard, my pulse spiked.

Many survivors call this "the curse of awareness." You notice everything but never feel safe.

To cope, I built a life of constant doing. Achievement was my anesthesia. Alcohol became my tranquilizer. Busyness kept the memories quiet until it didn't.

Trauma can also drive isolation. You avoid relationships because they feel dangerous, or you cling to unhealthy ones because loneliness feels worse. I did both. I would pull people close, then push them away the moment I sensed disappointment.

I wasn't being difficult. I was trying to control the one thing I never could as a child: the moment of abandonment.

Why Doctors Miss It

In my twenties and thirties, I saw a dozen doctors for symptoms ranging from migraines to stomach pain to fatigue. I took sleep aids, painkillers, and anxiety medication. Not one of them asked me about my childhood.

Most doctors are trained to treat the symptom, not the story behind it.

When your lab results are normal, yet your body feels anything but that, it's easy to start believing the lie that it's "all in your head."

But here's what I've learned: it's not all in your head. It's also in your nervous system, your hormones, your muscles, and your cells. The body and soul are not separate; they are one conversation happening in different languages.

That's why trauma-informed care matters. Healing isn't just about talking through memories; it's about teaching the body that the danger has passed.

Faith and the Body

For a long time, I was angry at my body. I thought it betrayed me, with pain, fatigue, and panic attacks. But eventually, I realized it had never betrayed me. It had protected me.

My body stayed alert so that little boy could survive. It braced, flinched, ran, and endured. It did exactly what God designed it to do in danger.

Now, as an adult, the task is different. My job is to teach it what peace feels like.

"Do you not know that your bodies are temples of the Holy Spirit, who is in you, whom you have received from God?" — 1 Corinthians 6:19

That verse once filled me with guilt. Now it fills me with awe. My body isn't my enemy. It is a temple that has been through war and still stands.

The Slow Theft of Joy

C-PTSD doesn't just steal health; it steals joy. It numbs you.

I remember sitting at my son's baseball game one sunny afternoon. He hit a double, the crowd cheered, and I smiled, but inside, I felt nothing. My mind was in the stands, but my heart was locked in some invisible room miles away.

That's the cost of dissociation. Your body is present, but your soul is still hiding.

For years, I mistook that numbness for strength. I thought it meant I had control. But numbness isn't control. It is absence. Healing began when I stopped trying to numb out and started daring to feel again, even when those feelings hurt.

Survivor Insight: Recognizing the Body's Alarm System

Notice patterns, not just moments. If you always tense up in certain situations, your body is speaking.

Track your triggers. Keep a small notebook. Write what happened right before your anxiety spiked.

Reframe pain as communication. Ask, "What is my body trying to tell me?"

Be gentle. The goal isn't to silence symptoms; it is to understand them.

Quick Win: The 5-4-3-2-1 Grounding Reset

When your body goes into panic or freeze mode, use your senses to come back to the present.

5 – Name five things you can see.

4 – Name four things you can touch.

3 – Name three things you can hear.

2 – Name two things you can smell.

1 – Name one thing you can taste.

This simple exercise rewires your nervous system to recognize safety. It isn't magic. It is biology. It activates the part of your brain that says, "I'm here, and I'm safe right now."

Learning to Live in a Healed Body

Today, my body still carries scars, both physical and emotional, but I see them differently.

Where I once saw weakness, I now see witness. My body is evidence that God can carry a person through anything and still let them stand.

Some mornings I still wake tense, but instead of fighting it, I breathe, pray, and remind myself: That was then; this is now.

Healing doesn't mean the absence of symptoms. It means the presence of grace in the middle of them.

"He gives strength to the weary and increases the power of the weak." — Isaiah 40:29

Closing Reflection

If trauma steals your life one symptom at a time, recovery gives it back one breath at a time.

Every time you pause before reacting, every moment you choose rest over rushing, every prayer whispered in the middle of panic, that is healing.

Your body isn't the enemy. It is the survivor.

It is the temple where God has been working quietly all along.

The same body that once flinched in fear can someday relax in peace.

The same mind that once raced with panic can someday rest in trust.

You are not crazy. You are not beyond repair.

You are a miracle in motion, proof that what was once wounded can still be wonderfully made.

CHAPTER 4

The Terrible Math of Trauma

Trauma has a strange way of keeping score. It tallies wounds quietly, often beneath the surface, adding one injury to another until the body can no longer ignore the sum. You don't see the arithmetic while you are living through it. You only recognize it years later, when the patterns come into focus like numbers finally lining up on a ledger you never realized you were keeping.

I call this phenomenon the terrible math of trauma, the way a single wound compounds into many, and how those many wounds seep into parts of your life you never expected to feel their reach. Trauma does not stay in one place. It multiplies. It adds. It sometimes divides. And for a long time, I didn't understand why.

I only understood the symptoms, not the equation.

The Ledger No One Told Me I Was Keeping

I first realized something deeper was happening when I was in my thirties, sitting in yet another doctor's office. I had come in because I was exhausted all the time, bone-deep exhaustion that no amount of sleep or vacation could fix. My blood pressure was high. My digestion was a mess. My muscles felt permanently clenched, as if they had forgotten how to let go.

The doctor ran tests. Everything came back "normal."

But I didn't feel normal.

I felt like I was carrying the weight of something invisible, something heavy enough to bend me in half. At the time, I didn't have the words for what I now know: trauma keeps financial books the way an accountant keeps numbers. Every fear you survived, every night you stayed awake listening for danger, every time your adrenaline spiked when someone raised their voice, those experiences were recorded somewhere inside you.

And eventually, the bill comes due.

The Science Behind the Weight

Understanding the biology of trauma changed my life. It helped me stop blaming myself for things that were never moral failings. They were physiological realities. Trauma alters the body's chemistry. It changes the brain's architecture. It reprograms the nervous system to survival mode.

Researchers call this "toxic stress," and it literally reshapes the developing brain.

The amygdala, the alarm bell of the mind, becomes enlarged and triggers more easily.

The prefrontal cortex, responsible for logic and decision-making, has trouble regulating the emotional storm.

The hippocampus, which processes memory, shrinks under prolonged stress, making it harder to distinguish past threats from present safety.

I didn't know any of this growing up. I only knew that I startled easily, slept lightly, and lived as though danger was always one moment away. I couldn't understand why my reactions were so outsized compared to the situations around me.

Now I know the truth: my brain wasn't malfunctioning. It was doing its job too well.

It had learned to survive by becoming hypervigilant.

The Body Keeps Score — and It Keeps Interest

As I grew older, trauma's math began to show up in my body. My back pain grew worse. Headaches came more frequently. My heart raced at unpredictable times. My digestive system rebelled against me. I began to have chest tightness so severe that I went to the ER thinking I might be having a heart attack.

The tests always said the same thing:

"You're fine."

But I wasn't fine.

I was terrified, exhausted, and confused.

Trauma manifests physically because the body stores memories differently than the mind. The body remembers what you tried to forget. And when the body has spent decades expecting danger, it doesn't know how to live without fear.

This is why so many trauma survivors say, "I don't know why I feel this way."

The truth is, your body knows.

It has been carrying the math of your past long before you were able to understand the numbers.

"THE SCIENCE BEHIND…"

The Science Behind Emotional Flashbacks

Emotional flashbacks don't always contain clear memories.

Often, the body replays the feeling of past danger without visuals.

This happens because:

- The amygdala fires before conscious thought
- The hippocampus (memory center) is under-functioning
- The prefrontal cortex shuts down under threat

This creates moments where your body reacts to the present as if it were the past.

The Science Behind "Why I Shut Down"

Freezing is not weakness. It's biology.

When escape isn't possible, the nervous system goes into immobility:

- Muscles lose mobility
- Speech becomes difficult
- Emotions go numb
- Decision-making shuts down

> This is a biological survival strategy, not a character flaw.
>
> **The Science Behind Misdiagnosis**
> C-PTSD frequently mimics:
> - ADHD
> - Anxiety
> - Depression
> - Bipolar disorder
> - Personality disorders
>
> Why?
> Because chronic trauma alters:
> - Attention
> - Emotional regulation
> - Impulse control
> - Sleep
> - Hormones
> - Social responses
>
> Without childhood history, clinicians often see the symptoms, not the cause.

Trauma's Silent Equation:
Stress + Time = Breakdown

One of the most devastating forms of trauma math is the equation that emerges when you add stress over long periods of time. When the nervous system is constantly flooded with cortisol and adrenaline, the whole body ages faster.

Doctors now say that chronic childhood trauma can shorten lifespan by up to twenty years.

When I first heard that statistic, I felt a wave of shock, and then recognition. My body had felt older than my years for most of my life. I had been dealing with issues usually found in people decades older.

Trauma's math had been shaping me long before I knew how to calculate it.

The worst part? I thought it was all my fault.

I thought I was weak.

I thought I was too anxious.

I thought I wasn't "handling life" as well as everyone else.

But the truth was much simpler:

I wasn't failing.

I was injured.

The Descent Into Coping: When the Numbers Don't Add Up

Another equation trauma creates is the coping loop, the one many survivors know all too well.

For me, it started subtly. A drink at the end of a long day became two. Then three. Then more. I wasn't drinking to have fun. I was drinking to quiet the noise inside me, the racing thoughts, the tension, the fear that surged at random, the memories I didn't want to face, and the emotional spirals I didn't understand.

At the time, I told myself, "Everyone unwinds this way."

But deep down, I knew this wasn't unwinding. It was numbing.

Numbing is different from relaxing.

Numbing is survival.

Trauma math always finds a way to multiply when left untreated.

The Relational Costs: People Pay the Price Too

Trauma doesn't stop at the body. It finds its way into relationships, often in ways you don't see coming.

When you grow up walking on eggshells, you assume every conflict will explode.

When you grow up being criticized, you assume every negative tone means disapproval.

When you grow up waiting for the storm, you brace even during calm moments.

In my marriage, the wounds showed themselves the moment love felt too close. Love felt dangerous. Vulnerability felt reckless. When my wife expressed frustration or confusion, my chest tightened as if I were back in my childhood home anticipating an eruption.

I wasn't reacting to her.

I was reacting to the past.

This is one of trauma's cruelest mathematical tricks:

It makes you relive the wounds not with the people who caused them, but with the people who didn't.

It wasn't fair to my wife.

But it also wasn't because I didn't love her.

It was because my nervous system hadn't learned the difference between intimacy and danger.

Trauma multiplies fear, and fear divides relationships, often unintentionally.

The Equation of Achievement as Armor

Another manifestation of trauma math is the perfectionism that becomes armor. I learned early that mistakes were dangerous, so as an adult I worked relentlessly to avoid them. I excelled academically. I built a successful career. I studied, practiced, achieved, and performed as though my life depended on it.

In a way, it did.

Success became my shield.

Performance became my safety.

Achievement became my proof that I deserved to exist.

Externally, it looked like ambition.

Internally, it was fear.

People praised my discipline, not knowing that the cost was exhaustion, anxiety attacks, and a crushing internal standard I could never meet.

Trauma teaches you that being impressive is safer than being authentic.

Faith in the Middle of the Equation

For a long time, I thought God was disappointed in me. I thought my fear meant a lack of faith, and my symptoms meant I wasn't trusting Him enough. But as I learned more about trauma, I began to see God's presence in my story in a new light.

Scripture took on new meaning:

"God is our refuge and strength, an ever-present help in trouble." — Psalm 46:1

Ever-present.

Not after you heal.

Not once you get it together.

Not once you are no longer triggered.

Ever-present, even inside the fear you cannot explain.

God wasn't asking me to "stop being anxious."

He was whispering, "I'm with you inside the anxiety."

Hope doesn't erase trauma's math, but it does change the outcome.

The Moments That Shift the Numbers

Healing doesn't happen all at once. Instead, it happens in small turning points, moments when you begin to rewrite the equations that once felt inevitable.

For me, some of those moments were simple: realizing that my panic attacks weren't signs of weakness but signs of overload; understanding that my hypervigilance wasn't my personality but my protection; recognizing that my drinking wasn't rebellion but relief.

Other moments were profound: the burglary that shook me awake spiritually, the first time I admitted I needed help, the moment I walked into therapy and told the truth instead of the polished version of myself.

Those moments didn't subtract the trauma.

They started dividing its power.

They changed the trajectory of the numbers.

A Simple List, When Words Aren't Enough

Only a few lists truly belong in this chapter, and here are two.

Where Trauma Adds Up
- Emotional overwhelm
- Physical tension
- Survival-driven coping
- Relationship strain
- Shame and self-blame

Where Healing Divides the Weight
- Understanding the science
- Naming the truth
- Allowing support
- Practicing nervous system regulation
- Trusting God with the process

These two lists sum up the shift from living in trauma's mathematics to living in God's realm.

Healing Is God's New Math

Looking back on my life, I see the patterns now with a clarity I never had before. The fear, the exhaustion, the striving, the shame, all of it made sense through the lens of trauma. And once I understood the math, I could finally challenge the equations.

Healing didn't change the past.

But it changed the story the past told about me.

It changed the numbers that once defined my body, my mind, my relationships, and my future. And above all, it showed me that trauma doesn't get the last calculation. God does.

Where trauma multiplied wounds, God multiplied grace.

Where trauma divided connection, God restored it.

Where trauma subtracted hope, God added it back in abundance.

The terrible math of trauma is real.

But so is the holy math of healing.

And in the end, God's healing always wins.

PART THREE:
The Tangled Puppet Strings

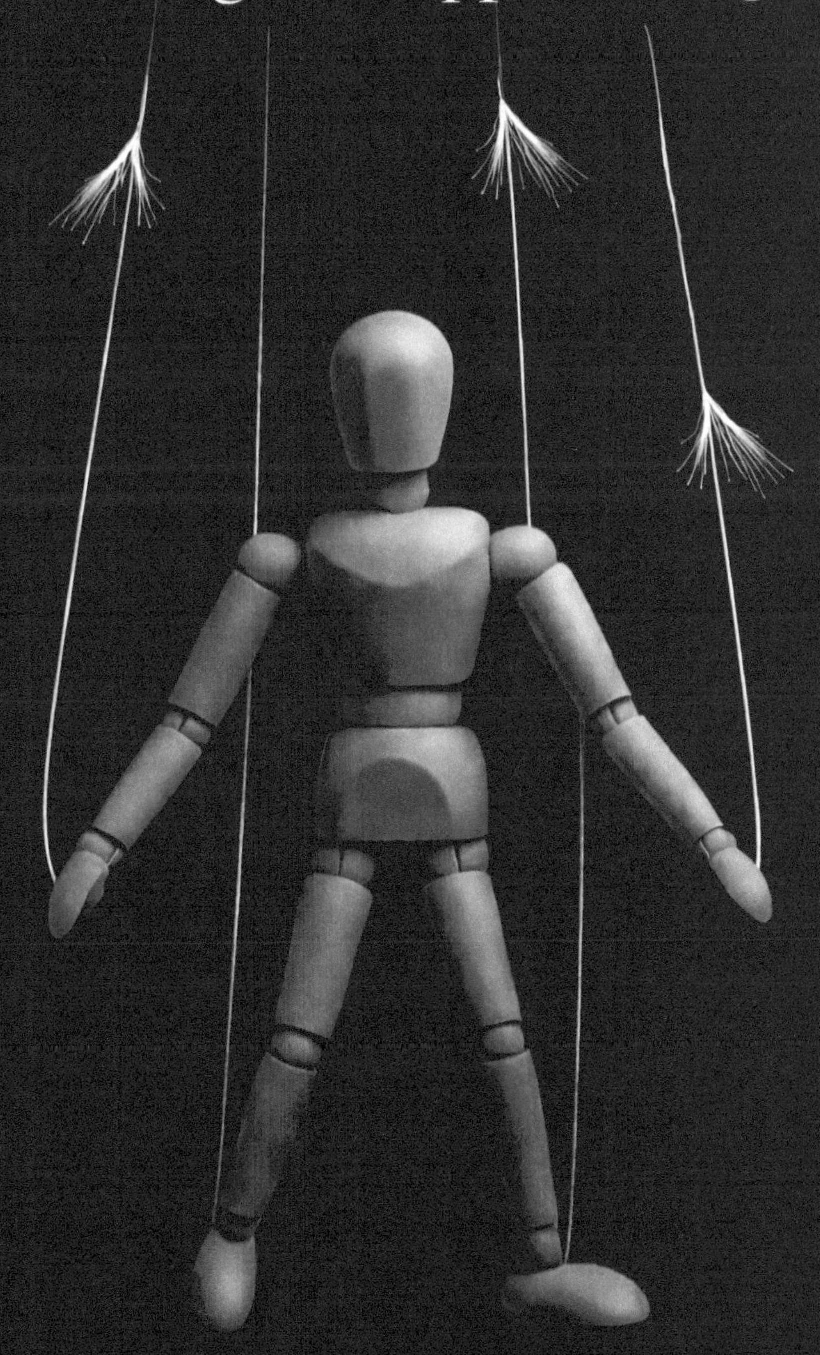

CHAPTER 5

Why Can't I Just Get Over It?

There is a question I've carried for most of my life, sometimes quietly, sometimes desperately, sometimes angrily:

Why can't I just get over it?

Why can't I stop reacting? Why can't I calm down? Why can't I let go of things that happened decades ago? Why can't I respond like other people do?

For years, I believed the answer was personal failure. I believed I lacked discipline. I believed I wasn't trying hard enough. I believed something inside me was fundamentally flawed. What I didn't know was that trauma creates reactions long before it creates understanding. Trauma wires the body for survival first and clarity later. And the gap between those two can feel like eternity.

Healing began when I finally learned the truth:

You don't "get over" trauma because trauma isn't a memory; it's a survival pattern your body learned to protect you.

The Brain That Won't Stand Down

When the body senses danger, the amygdala flips into high alert. It doesn't ask for permission or wait for your logical mind to catch up. It reacts instantly. It floods the system with stress hormones. It tenses muscles. It speeds up your heart. It prepares you to run or fight or freeze.

This is a brilliant design when danger is real. But when danger is recurring, as it is in a chaotic or abusive home, the alarm system becomes overly sensitive. A slammed door, a raised voice, even a certain expression can trigger the same cascades of fear the child once felt.

My body didn't forget those patterns. Its job was to keep me alive, not to keep me comfortable. As an adult, I still reacted to situations that were safe as though they were life-threatening. My nervous system couldn't distinguish past from present.

I wasn't being dramatic.

I wasn't being emotional.

I wasn't being weak.

I was being wired by years of survival.

And wiring doesn't change because you "try harder."

It changes because you understand it, work with it, and gently retrain it.

Harvard: When Pressure Meets Old Wounds

My time at Harvard was the perfect storm for someone with an overactive survival system. On the outside, it looked like the pinnacle of success. On the inside, it was a place where every insecurity, every wound, and every deeply buried fear rose to the surface.

The academic pressure alone could overwhelm anyone. But for me, it wasn't just pressure; it was activation. The expectations, the pace, and the scrutiny all hit the same neural pathways that had formed in childhood. My brain didn't see intellectual challenge. It saw danger.

I remember walking into McCollum Hall each morning with a knot in my stomach. The room would buzz with conversation, students preparing for discussions, debating strategy, comparing insights.

When hundreds of eyes turned toward me, the alarm bell rang in my chest. My palms would sweat. My vision would narrow. My breathing would quicken. Suddenly I wasn't in a classroom anymore. I was back in the emotional unpredictability of childhood, waiting for something to explode.

Inside, I was terrified of being embarrassed, rejected, or exposed. Those weren't academic fears; they were trauma fears.

To everyone else, it probably looked like I was pausing thoughtfully before answering.

Inside, I was fighting for breath.

I didn't understand why I reacted this way. All I saw was failure. All I felt was shame.

But now I understand: my reactions weren't about Harvard; they were about my history.

The Mask of Perfection

Like many trauma survivors, I learned early that perfection is protection. If I stayed ahead of everything, if I anticipated every problem, if I excelled at every task, maybe I could prevent disaster. Maybe I could prevent anger. Maybe I could earn safety.

At Harvard, this coping mechanism intensified. I believed that if I wasn't the smartest or the most prepared, I would be exposed. The stakes felt existential. I wasn't just afraid of failing an assignment; I was afraid of being seen as inadequate, which in my childhood meant vulnerability to harm.

So I worked tirelessly. I over-prepared. I studied late into the night even when I already understood the material. I tried to read every mood in the classroom, every shift in tone, every micro-reaction from professors.

I wasn't trying to succeed.

I was trying to survive.

Trauma makes performance feel like safety.

But it also makes rest feel like danger.

The perfection wasn't confidence.

It was fear wearing a suit.

The Loneliness of Success

People often assume that being surrounded by brilliant peers is energizing. But if you grew up never feeling safe, being around others, even good people, can feel like walking a tightrope without a net.

Harvard was full of opportunities for connection. Study groups, social events, group projects, late-night conversations in the common rooms. But I rarely let myself participate. I hung back. I appeared friendly but kept my distance. My classmates were kind, but kindness was unfamiliar. Vulnerability felt impossible.

I felt isolated even in crowded rooms because I didn't know how to be known.

I didn't know how to trust that being myself wouldn't result in hurt.

I didn't know how to stop performing long enough to let anyone in.

Loneliness isn't the absence of people; it's the absence of safety.

And trauma creates both.

Red Flags That Trauma Is Running the Show
- You overreact to minor criticism
- Loud noises make your chest tighten
- You over-explain to avoid upsetting people
- You "crash" after conflict, even small conflicts
- You numb out instead of feeling
- You're terrified of someone being disappointed
- You forget parts of conversations during stress

Green Flags of Healing
You pause before reacting
- Your spirals shorten
- You can name your triggers
- You apologize without shame
- Healthy people feel safer than they used to
- You can rest without guilt (even for a moment)
- You catch yourself speaking kindly to yourself

The Spirals: When the Body Takes Over

One of the most painful parts of living with C-PTSD is how quickly the nervous system can hijack the moment. A tone of voice, a facial expression, a misunderstanding, anything that resembles past danger, sends the amygdala into overdrive.

When a spiral hits, the brain stops processing information effectively. It floods with emotion. Thoughts become catastrophic. Shame intensifies. The ability to think clearly shuts down.

I had spirals while at Harvard. I had spirals in my marriage. I had spirals at work. I didn't understand why they were happening. I didn't know they were emotional flashbacks, reliving feelings from childhood without conscious memories attached.

It took years to understand that during a spiral, the body isn't asking for analysis. It's asking for safety.

Why Willpower Isn't Enough

This is one of the most important lessons I learned:

Trauma lives in the body. Willpower lives in the mind.

In moments of overwhelm, I used to force myself to "get it together." Now I understand that respecting my survival system is the first step to transforming it.

The nervous system isn't your enemy. It is a child who learned to survive without guidance. It needs reassurance, not reprimand. It needs calm, not criticism. It needs patience, not pressure.

Trauma's Puppet Strings

Trauma acts like invisible strings, pulling reactions out of you before your mind can intervene.

You dissociate.

You overcompensate.

Not because you're dramatic or unstable, but because the past still lives inside your body.

These strings don't make you weak. They make you wounded.

And wounds can heal.

The Faith That Held Me Together

During my darkest moments, I often returned to a simple prayer:

"God, be with me in this."

Sometimes that was all I could manage.

I used to believe God was disappointed in my fear. I thought my anxiety meant I lacked trust. But over time, Scripture showed me a different picture of God, not a judge waiting for me to overcome, but a Father walking with me through the fear.

When I read, "My grace is sufficient for you," I finally understood that grace wasn't a reward for doing better. It was support for the moments when I couldn't.

God didn't ask me to be fearless.

He asked me to let Him in.

And that changed everything.

Two Small Lists That Matter

What Trauma Makes You Believe

- "Something is wrong with me."

- "Everyone else handles life better than I do."

- "I should be over this by now."

What Healing Helps You Understand

- "My reactions make sense given my past."

- "My nervous system is trying to protect me."

- "I can heal at my own pace."

These truths create space for compassion, toward yourself and your story.

Rewiring Doesn't Mean Forgetting

Healing isn't erasing the past. It is teaching the body a new language.

It is slowing your breathing when the alarm goes off.

It is grounding yourself when fear rises.

It is reminding your nervous system that the danger is over.

It is allowing love to break through the walls that once kept you safe.

Healing is the work of a lifetime, not because you're damaged, but because you're learning how to live in a world your body no longer has to fear.

Closing Reflection

For years, I begged myself to "just get over it." I blamed myself for every reaction, every outburst, every moment of panic.

I mistook symptoms for identity. I mistook survival responses for failures.

Now I understand:

You don't get over trauma.

You get through it.

You walk with it.

You heal layer by layer.

You learn your nervous system's language and teach it a new one.

You stop fighting your reactions and start comforting them.

You stop shaming the frightened parts of you and start listening to them.

Healing isn't about forgetting. It is about remembering with compassion.

Healing isn't about toughness. It is about tenderness.

Healing isn't about erasing trauma. It is about rewriting its meaning.

You're not stuck because you're weak.

You're stuck because you're wounded.

And wounds heal, not by force, but by care.

You cannot "just get over it."

But you can grow through it.

And with truth, patience, and God's presence, you will.

CHAPTER 6

Misdiagnosis Roulette

By the time someone finally spoke the words Complex Post-Traumatic Stress Disorder to me, I had already collected a decade's worth of diagnoses that each explained a fragment of my life but never the whole picture. I felt like I was spinning a wheel at every appointment, waiting to see which label it would land on next. Sometimes it stopped on anxiety, sometimes on depression, sometimes on ADHD, sometimes on something scarier. Each one made sense in its own way, but none of them tied everything together.

What I didn't know then was that trauma hides behind other labels. It mimics them. It imitates them. It can look like almost anything except what it actually is. Trauma is the great chameleon of mental health. And when you don't know your history is the root, you end up treating every branch individually, never realizing all the branches are growing from the same wounded tree.

For years, I thought I was broken. But the truth was simpler:

I wasn't broken. I was misdiagnosed.

Diagnosis #1: "You Have Anxiety"

My first misdiagnosis came in my twenties, during a time when my body felt like it was constantly buzzing. My heart raced for no reason. My palms were always sweaty. My mind jumped from one fear to the next. Sleep came in fragments. I didn't know how to relax without feeling guilty or unsafe.

A doctor listened, nodded, and said, "This is classic anxiety."

He wasn't wrong—not entirely. I did have anxiety.

But he never asked why.

No one asked about my childhood. No one asked about the environment I grew up in. No one asked about the constant fear I lived under as a kid. To them, anxiety was a standalone condition, not a symptom. Not a clue.

I walked out of his office with a prescription but without answers. The medication helped the edges but not the core. It took the panic from a ten down to a seven, but the underlying storm was still brewing.

Diagnosis #2: "You're Probably Depressed"

A year later, when anxiety treatment didn't fix everything, a new provider decided I might be depressed. I didn't fit the stereotype of depression. I wasn't bedridden. I wasn't lethargic. I didn't withdraw from people. I wasn't hopeless.

But I was numb.

There were days when I felt nothing at all, no joy, no sadness, no excitement, no fear. Just blank. Like someone had turned the dimmer switch down on my emotional world.

That flattening of emotion wasn't depression; it was survival. When you grow up in chaos, your body learns to shut down feelings as a form of protection. Emotional numbness becomes a shield against overwhelming pain.

But no one explained that to me then.

They just called it depression and adjusted the medication.

That's the cruel thing about misdiagnosis. The treatment can become a source of shame. When you're given the wrong label, you begin to believe you're failing at getting better.

Diagnosis #3: "It Might Be ADHD"

In my early thirties, another possibility emerged. I couldn't focus. My thoughts scattered easily. I procrastinated, not because I was lazy, but because I didn't know how to start tasks without spiraling. I lost items constantly. My mind jumped between worries, ideas, responsibilities, and noises, always scanning.

A clinician suggested ADHD.

It made sense on the surface. I had the symptoms. But again, no one connected the symptoms to the story behind them.

Later I learned something that made everything click:

Trauma can look exactly like ADHD.

When your nervous system is overstimulated, sustained attention becomes a luxury. The brain becomes wired for scanning, not focusing. The mind hops from thought to thought because it is always preparing for threat.

Medication helped with concentration but made me even more anxious. I thought that side effect meant something was wrong with me. Now I know it simply meant I didn't have ADHD. I had trauma.

Diagnosis #4: "This Looks Like Bipolar Disorder"

The most frightening diagnosis came during a period of intense stress. I was overwhelmed, reactive, and up at night battling racing thoughts. My energy spiked some days and cratered others. I felt emotionally volatile.

A clinician looked at my symptoms and said, "You may have bipolar disorder."

That word terrified me. It felt heavy, ominous, irreversible. I walked out of that appointment with a knot in my stomach, feeling as though my life had just been split in two.

Years later, I discovered something that brought both relief and anger:

C-PTSD can look just like bipolar disorder.

The difference is that trauma responses are triggered, while bipolar episodes are cyclical.

No one asked what triggered mine.

No one asked what my childhood was like.

No one asked about the fear I carried daily.

Misdiagnosis is more than an error. It is a wound. Being told "you might be bipolar" when you are actually traumatized creates layers of unnecessary shame and confusion.

FIVE QUICK WIN EXERCISES
(5-Minute Nervous System Resets)

Quick Win #1: 5-4-3-2-1 Grounding Reset

Use your senses to return to the present:

5 – things you see

4 – things you can touch

3 – sounds you hear

2 – things you can smell

1 – thing you can taste

Use anytime spirals begin.

Quick Win #2: The 60-Second Breath Ladder

Breathe in for 4 seconds

Hold for 2

Exhale for 6

Repeat for one minute.

This signals safety to the vagus nerve.

Quick Win #3: The Weighted Blanket Trick (Without a Blanket)

Sit in a chair.

Press your feet firmly into the floor.

Place your hands flat on your thighs.

Apply gentle downward pressure.

This engages proprioception, the body's internal GPS, and reduces hyperarousal.

Quick Win #4: The "Name the Fear" Technique
When anxiety spikes, say:
"This is fear. I have felt this before. It will pass."
This pulls the amygdala's power into the rational brain.

Quick Win #5: Cold Temperature Reset
Run cool water over your hands or splash your face.
This activates the mammalian dive reflex and calms your system within seconds.

The Therapist Who Finally Asked the Right Question

After a decade of incorrect labels, I finally met a clinician who didn't rush to conclusions. He listened to my symptoms, panic, hypervigilance, numbness, people-pleasing, perfectionism, spirals, and instead of reaching for his diagnostic manual, he asked a question no one had asked before.

"John... what was home like when you were growing up?"

I froze.

No provider had ever asked me about my childhood. But that one question opened a door that changed my life. As I described the unpredictability, the shouting, the fear, the bracing-for-impact reality I lived with as a kid, his expression shifted with recognition.

When I finished, he said gently, "Everything you've described points to Complex PTSD."

For the first time, I felt seen, truly seen.

Not as a cluster of symptoms.

Not as a difficult case.

Not as a misfit.

I felt understood.

I wasn't someone with ten different disorders.

I was someone with one unhealed wound.

And that wound was finally being named.

Why Trauma Gets Misdiagnosed So Easily

Trauma is one of the most camouflaged conditions in mental health. It hides behind other symptoms because its effects touch every part of the body. It affects attention, emotion, memory, behavior, relationships, sleep, immunity, and spirituality.

That is why it is mistaken for so many other things.

Trauma can mirror anxiety.

Trauma can mirror depression.

Trauma can mirror ADHD.

Trauma can mirror bipolar disorder.

Trauma can mirror personality disorders.

In short, trauma can look like everything except itself.

This is why diagnosis without understanding the person's history is like reading a book by only looking at the last chapter. You miss the story that explains everything.

The Emotional Cost of Misdiagnosis

Being misdiagnosed doesn't just delay healing. It deepens pain.

Every incorrect label made me believe I was failing.

Every unsuccessful treatment made me believe I was broken.

Every moment I didn't improve made me believe I wasn't trying hard enough.

Misdiagnosis left me feeling ashamed of reactions that made perfect sense once the full story came to light. It made me think my symptoms were signs of weakness instead of signs of injury.

When you treat trauma like a character flaw, you lose years to self-blame.

Faith Reframed the Picture

Through all the confusion, Scripture became a lifeline. Not as a cliché, but as a lens. Verses I had read my whole life began to land differently.

"The Lord is near to the brokenhearted."

"He heals the crushed in spirit."

"My grace is sufficient for you."

"I am with you always."

I started to see God not as someone waiting for me to overcome my issues, but as someone sitting with me inside them.

It was never "Why can't you fix this?"

It was "Let's walk through this together."

Grace didn't erase the misdiagnoses.

It healed the shame they caused.

A Short List, When a List Matters

What Misdiagnosis Does to a Survivor

- It delays the true healing process.
- It reinforces the belief that something is inherently wrong with you.
- It can worsen symptoms by giving you the wrong tools.

What the Correct Diagnosis Can Do

- It replaces shame with understanding.
- It replaces confusion with clarity.
- It opens the door to the right kind of healing.

Sometimes lists bring clarity to the chaos.

Finding the Right Path

Once I understood I had C-PTSD, everything made sense. My panic wasn't random. My shutdowns weren't personality flaws. My reactions weren't dramatic. My difficulty with conflict wasn't immaturity. My fear wasn't because I lacked faith.

All of it was the inevitable result of a childhood spent surviving instead of growing.

Naming the truth was the first step toward reclaiming my life.

Healing wasn't instantaneous. It was slow, steady, intentional. But it was real. And with clarity came compassion, for myself, for the frightened child I once was, and for the adult who carried those wounds into every corner of life.

Understanding the root gave me permission to stop fighting myself and start healing myself.

Closing Reflection

If you have spent years feeling misunderstood, mislabeled, or ashamed of symptoms that never quite fit the boxes people tried to put you in, I want you to hear this clearly:

You are not crazy.

You are not weak.

You are not failing.

You may simply be misdiagnosed.

The day someone finally names the wound is the day the healing begins.

The day the story makes sense is the day shame starts to lift.

And the day you realize trauma shaped your reactions is the day you stop blaming yourself for having them.

You cannot heal what has not been named.

But once it is named, everything changes.

PART FOUR:
The Road to Healing

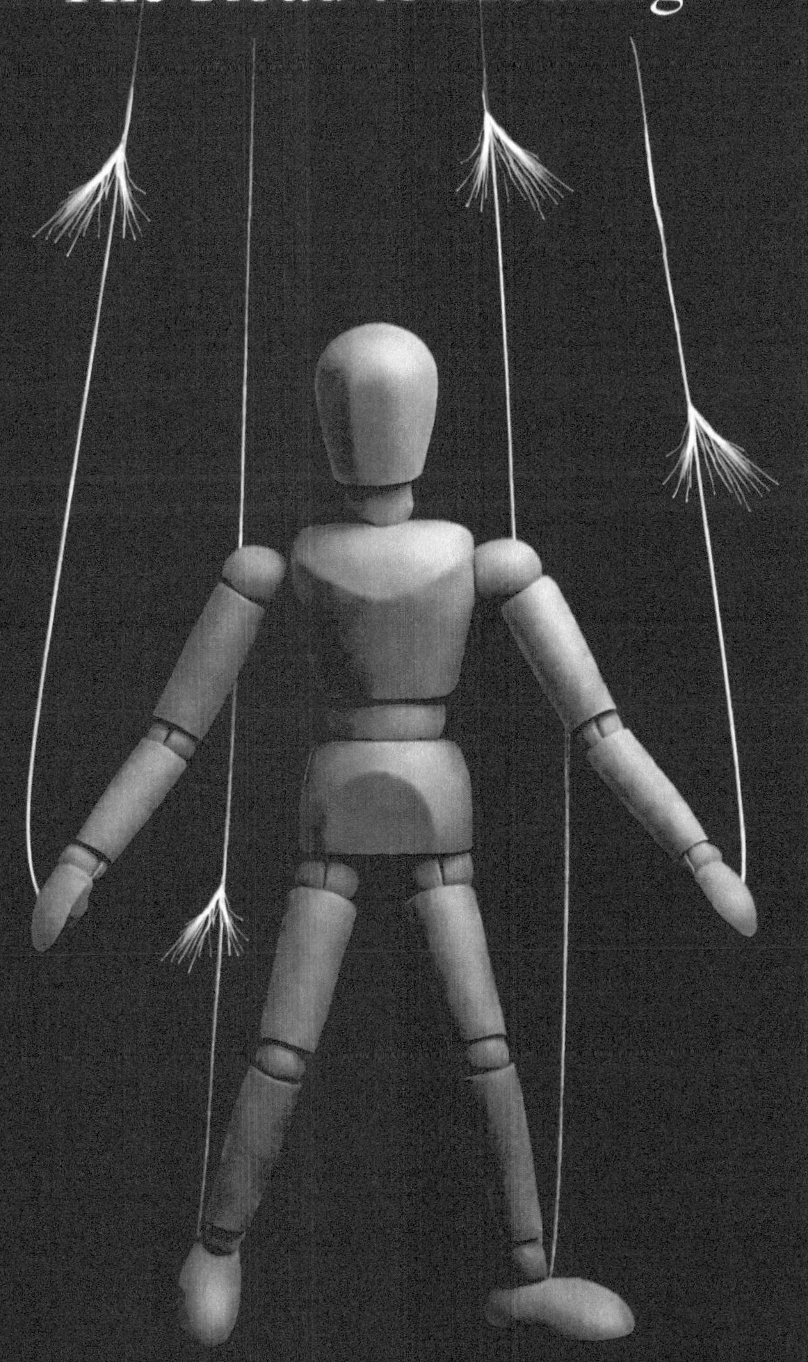

CHAPTER 7

Finding Your Lifelines

One of the most profound truths about trauma is that it isolates. It convinces you that you are alone, that no one will understand your pain, that your struggles are yours to carry, and yours alone. For most of my life, I believed that lie. I believed I had to handle everything myself. I believed that relying on others was weakness. I believed asking for help made me a burden. And I believed those things because I grew up in an environment where needing anything was unsafe.

But healing taught me a different truth: none of us are meant to heal alone. Every major breakthrough in my life came because God placed a lifeline in my path, a person who saw me, supported me, challenged me, or simply stayed when it would have been easier to walk away. When trauma pulls you under, lifelines keep you afloat long enough to breathe again.

In this chapter, I want to honor those lifelines. I want to show how they appeared, often without announcement, often in quiet moments, often disguised as ordinary people doing ordinary things that ended up changing my life. And I want to show how healing becomes possible when you finally allow yourself to be carried by others.

The First Lifeline: Being Seen as a Child

My earliest lifelines came long before I knew what a lifeline was. They came during the years when home felt dangerous and unpredictable. As a child, I didn't have the language to describe my fear. I didn't know how to tell anyone what was happening. I just knew that some adults felt safe and others didn't.

One of my first lifelines was Dr. Lane, my dorm parent in boarding school. I don't know how much he saw or understood, but he saw enough. He saw the tension in my shoulders, the guarded way I answered questions, the discomfort in my eyes when certain topics came up. He never pressed me, never forced me to talk, but he made me feel calm simply by the way he spoke to me. He treated me with dignity at an age when I felt invisible at home.

I remember one day when he placed his hand gently on my arm after an appointment and said, "You're a strong kid, John. Stronger than you realize." I carried those words for years. They felt like armor. They felt like possibility. They felt like someone believed something about me that I didn't yet believe about myself.

Years later, I realized the significance: every child who lives in chaos needs one safe adult who sees them clearly. Sometimes that single person becomes the difference between despair and survival.

The Teachers Who Became Anchors

As I got older, teachers became my next lifelines. They didn't know the full story, but they sensed something beneath the surface, something fragile, something scared, something needing encouragement. They didn't fix me, but they believed in me.

One of the most significant figures was Mrs. Kozub. She could see beyond the mask of performance and humor I used to protect myself. She noticed that I always volunteered to help, worked hard, and seemed overly concerned with getting things right. One day after class, she pulled me aside and said, "You don't have to carry everything alone."

Those eight words landed deeper than she could have known. I didn't know how to stop carrying everything, but her compassion planted a seed. It told me that maybe there were people who could share my load. Maybe I didn't have to carry fear and shame by myself. Maybe support was something people gave freely, without expecting anything in return.

The Brothers I Found Along the Way

As I matured and began navigating adulthood, new lifelines appeared in the form of friendships that shaped me in unexpected ways. Men like Moose, Jeff, and Kiley entered my life at different times, but each of them helped me confront pieces of my story I had spent years avoiding.

Moose became one of my first examples of steady masculinity, the kind that is strong without being intimidating, protective without being controlling, confident without being aggressive. Growing up, I had never experienced healthy male leadership. Most of the male energy in my home was unpredictable or frightening. Moose's presence helped rewrite that script. He became a reminder that not all men explode when frustrated, not all men lead with fear, and not all men need to dominate to feel powerful.

Jeff showed me what honesty looks like. He wasn't afraid to talk about his emotions. He wasn't ashamed to admit when life was too much. His openness gave me permission to be more open myself. When trauma teaches you to hide everything, honesty from someone else feels like an invitation to breathe.

And then there was Kiley, who had a gift for reflecting truth back to me. He saw strengths I didn't recognize, talents I dismissed, and worth I didn't believe I had. Lifelines come in many forms. Some rescue you by pulling you out of danger, and others rescue you by showing you the parts of yourself you have forgotten.

These friendships didn't heal my trauma, but they softened it. They made space for vulnerability to emerge where I once felt only fear.

Marriage: The Lifeline That Revealed My Wounds

Marriage to my wife Kyla became one of the most honest mirrors in my healing journey. Loving someone deeply brings buried wounds to the surface. It reveals the hidden triggers, the fears, the patterns, and the places where your nervous system still holds the past.

My wife walked through all of that with me. She saw the panic behind my eyes when conflict arose. She saw how I shut down when emotions were too intense. She saw the overreactions that made no sense in the moment but made perfect sense in the context of my childhood.

There were times when my trauma hurt her, times when my shutdowns created distance between us, and times when I couldn't articulate what was happening inside me. But she stayed. She asked questions. She sought to understand rather than judge.

Loving someone with C-PTSD requires patience and grace. But being loved while healing from C-PTSD requires a different kind of courage, the courage to let yourself be known. My wife became a lifeline not because she healed me, but because she never walked away from the parts of me that still needed healing.

Her love was a steady reminder that connection is possible even after years of believing it wasn't.

Fatherhood: The Lifeline That Changed My Direction

When my sons, Jack and Anthony, came into the world, everything shifted. Becoming a father made my motivation to heal urgent. I didn't want my sons growing up in the shadow of my unresolved trauma. I wanted them to experience the safety, stability, and unconditional love I never had as a child.

Holding each of them for the first time felt like both a promise and a challenge. The promise was that love could be different, gentler, safer, and more present. The challenge was that I needed to become the kind of father I rarely saw modeled for me.

My boys didn't create my healing, but they inspired it. They became a daily reminder that breaking generational cycles isn't theoretical. It is lived out in small decisions, quiet moments, and choices to respond differently than how you were taught.

They didn't rescue me.

But they gave me a reason to rescue myself.

SEE IT

BREAKING GENERATIONAL CYCLES: BECOMING THE FATHER I NEVER HAD

Growing up, I didn't dream about becoming a father. Not because I didn't want children someday, but because the idea scared me. I had no roadmap, no model, no memory of what healthy fatherhood looked like. My childhood was filled with volatility, silence, and walking on eggshells. The idea of raising a child when I still felt like a scared kid inside myself seemed impossible. I carried a quiet fear for years, a fear that I would pass my trauma on. A fear that the tension, the shutdowns, the freezing, the panic, the overreactions would leak into my parenting. A fear that I would fail my children the way adults had once failed me.

The night my first son, Jack, was born, I remember standing in the hospital room holding him. He was tiny, pink, blinking up at me as if I were the only person in the world. And I felt two things at once: overwhelming love... and overwhelming fear.

What if I wasn't enough?

What if I lost my temper?

What if I shut down?

What if my past harmed my future?

But something else happened in that moment, something I didn't expect. As I held him, I felt a quiet conviction rise inside me, not a loud voice, not a dramatic revelation, just a gentle truth:

"The cycle ends with you."

It wasn't a promise of perfection. It wasn't a guarantee I wouldn't make mistakes. It was an invitation:

to parent differently,

to love differently,

to speak differently,

to be present in a way I never experienced.

When my second son, Anthony, was born, that conviction deepened. Becoming their father didn't erase my fear, but it transformed it. Instead of fearing I'd become my past, I feared what would happen if I didn't heal from it.

Fatherhood made my trauma urgent.

It forced me to confront parts of myself I had avoided.

It revealed wounds I didn't know were still raw.

But it also gave me a purpose strong enough to keep going, even when healing felt impossible.

There are days when my body reacts before my mind can catch up. A loud crash, a door slamming, a raised voice, old patterns still fire inside me. My sons have seen moments when I go quiet, when I take a breath, when I step into another room to calm my nervous system. But each time I return to them, present and grounded, I'm teaching them something I never learned: that emotions can be felt without being feared.

I used to worry that my wounds made me a worse father. Now I understand that my healing is what makes me a better one.

My boys will grow up knowing that strength doesn't mean silence.

They will grow up seeing repair, not rage.

They will grow up seeing a father who apologizes, who explains, who listens.

They will grow up knowing love isn't earned by perfection. It's given freely.

Healing as a parent isn't about erasing the past.

It's about refusing to pass it on.

And every time I choose connection instead of fear, gentleness instead of anger, courage instead of avoidance, I am building a different kind of legacy, one my sons can climb on instead of escape from.

God knew what He was doing when He made me their father. And I'm learning, slowly and surely, how to believe that too.

The Therapist Who Finally Held the Map

You can't navigate trauma alone. You can't see all your blind spots, you can't name every wound, and you can't dismantle the patterns you built for survival. That is why the doctor who diagnosed me with C-PTSD became one of the most important lifelines in my story.

He didn't rush me. He didn't overwhelm me. He didn't reduce me to symptoms. Instead, he helped me understand my reactions, my triggers, my shutdowns, and my attachment wounds with compassion.

He taught me what emotional flashbacks were. He taught me how to regulate my nervous system. He taught me how to differentiate past danger from present safety. And most importantly, he taught me that healing wasn't about becoming someone else. It was about becoming who I was always meant to be before trauma distorted the picture.

A skilled trauma specialist doesn't "fix" you.

They walk the path with you until you can walk parts of it on your own.

Why You Need Lifelines, Even If You Don't Want Them

Trauma is relational injury. Healing is relational restoration. The very thing that wounded you becomes the thing that heals you.

For many survivors, this truth is difficult to accept. Allowing people to get close to you feels terrifying. Trust feels reckless. Letting someone see the real you feels unsafe. But letting others in, slowly and carefully, is what begins to untangle the knots trauma created.

Lifelines don't take away your pain.

They prevent you from drowning in it.

How to Recognize a True Lifeline

Not everyone is meant to be part of your healing. Some people trigger old wounds. Some reinforce harmful patterns. Some are simply not equipped to walk through trauma with you.

But lifelines share certain qualities.

Here are the signs:
- They make you feel safe, not small.
- They listen more than they lecture.
- They offer compassion without pity.
- They stay present even when you're struggling.

When you find people like that, hold onto them. They are rare. They are gifts. They are evidence of God's care woven directly into your story.

The Faith Beneath All Other Lifelines

Every lifeline I have ever had, teachers, friends, mentors, my wife, my sons, my therapist, felt like they were placed in my life intentionally. Not randomly. Not accidentally. But by design.

When I look back, I can see God's fingerprints everywhere. He didn't prevent the trauma, but He never left me in it alone. He brought people into my life who reflected His steadiness, His compassion, His truth, His presence.

The verse that anchors this chapter for me is:

"Two are better than one, because they have a good return for their labor." — Ecclesiastes 4:9

God lifts us up, sometimes through prayer, sometimes through Scripture, but often through the hands and voices of the people He places in our lives.

Healing is rarely loud.

Often, it comes in the quiet presence of someone who stays.

A Short List for Survivors Looking for Support

How to Begin Letting Others In
- Start with one safe person.
- Share one honest sentence, not your entire story.
- Allow small acts of support before large ones.

This is how connection grows, slowly, gently, at a pace that honors your nervous system.

Closing Reflection

When I think about the lifelines God sent me, the teachers, the friends, the mentors, the trauma specialists, my wife, and my boys, I realize that healing was never a solo journey. Healing was a team effort, a divine collaboration between God and the people who answered His call to show up for me.

Trauma isolates, but lifelines reconnect. They remind you that you're not meant to carry everything alone. They show you that people can be safe. They help you rewrite a story you once believed was set in stone.

If you've spent your life believing you don't need anyone, or that no one would stay if they knew the real you, let this chapter be a gentle reminder:

You are worthy of support.

You are worthy of connection.

You are worthy of people who stay.

And whether you see it yet or not,

God is already sending your lifelines.

CHAPTER 8

Hope Changes Everything

Hope is a strange thing. When you're living under the weight of trauma, hope feels distant, fragile, and almost foreign. It is something other people talk about, something that belongs to people whose lives feel steady. For a long time, hope felt like a language I didn't speak. People told me things would get better, but those words felt like empty air compared to the heaviness inside me.

Yet hope has a way of creeping into the cracks, often without your permission. It slips into the moments where pain has left a little space, a sliver of light. I didn't find hope all at once. It found me slowly, in pieces, through people, through faith, through surrender, through moments I never expected to become turning points.

Hope didn't erase my past. It rewrote my future.

Healing Is Never Linear

For years, I believed healing should happen in a straight line. I thought if I learned enough, prayed enough, tried hard enough, or stayed positive enough, the pain would leave and peace would take its place. When that didn't happen, I assumed I was doing something wrong.

The truth is healing is rarely neat. It is circular, layered, and uneven. Some days you feel light and confident, certain you have turned a corner. Other days you feel like you have gone backward into old patterns you thought you had outgrown.

One therapist told me, "You're not backsliding. You're revisiting old wounds at a deeper level." That reframe changed everything. Instead of seeing myself as someone who couldn't get it right, I began to understand I was doing the brave work of healing in layers.

When trauma is complex and was learned through years of survival, healing takes time. Not because you are weak, but because your body spent years learning to survive, and it must now learn to live.

From the Bottom to Harvard:
A Story of Becoming

When I think about the trajectory of my life, from the frightened boy who hid in his room, to the young man who felt like an imposter, to the adult who walked into Harvard, it feels like two incompatible stories. How does someone who once believed he wasn't smart, lovable, or capable end up earning a place at one of the most prestigious institutions in the world?

Hope was the bridge between those two realities.

Hope came in the form of teachers who believed in me before I believed in myself. Hope came in the form of mentors who redirected my path. Hope came through the Kiski School, where structure and support finally allowed me to breathe. Hope came through moments where I pushed myself further than my fear wanted me to go.

But Harvard was not an arrival. It was a mirror. It forced me to confront the parts of myself I had avoided. It showed me that external success doesn't heal internal wounds. It showed me the facade of competence cannot erase the fears the heart holds onto.

Hope didn't mean I felt confident. Hope meant I kept showing up anyway.

The Breaking Point: Sobriety and Surrender

Addiction didn't appear in my life as rebellion. It appeared as relief. Alcohol numbed the panic, quieted the racing thoughts, and softened the edges of wounds I didn't yet know how to treat. It became a coping strategy, one that worked until it didn't.

There was a night in a hotel room that changed everything. I had just finished a work event where I had played the part everyone expected of me, the confident leader, the polished professional, the man who "had it all together." But when I returned to my room and the performance ended, the emptiness roared back. I sat staring at an empty glass, realizing I had spent years trying to outrun myself.

That night, I reached a breaking point, not the kind that destroys you, but the kind that finally humbles you into honesty. I whispered the most important prayer of my life: "God, I can't do this anymore. Please help me."

And He did.

Sobriety made space for hope.

Hope made space for healing.

Healing made space for purpose.

FIVE

THE KISKI TURNING POINT

Leaving home for Kiski Prep was the first time I ever realized safety could exist. I remember loading my father's Suburban that morning — my stomach in knots, my heart racing. Childhood had taught me to brace. Change felt like danger.

But Kiski was the first place where adults believed I was capable.

Teachers looked me in the eye.

They challenged me.

They pushed me without breaking me.

And for the first time, I wasn't surviving, I was learning.

My grades rose.

My confidence shifted.

My world expanded.

Kiski didn't erase my trauma, but it disrupted the cycle. It showed me what healthy support looked like. It planted the idea that I might actually become someone.

Sometimes healing begins the moment someone gives you the chance to rise.

The Burglary That Became a Spiritual Turning Point

There was another moment that deepened my understanding of hope, a moment that could have destroyed me but instead transformed me.

It was late at night when someone broke into our home. The sound shattered the silence, sending my nervous system into full alarm. For a moment, everything inside me reverted to childhood, the fear, the helplessness, the instinct to protect and hide.

But something else happened, something I have never fully been able to articulate. In the middle of terror, I felt an unexplainable calm wash over me. A sense of protection. A sense of Someone larger, steadier, stronger than fear itself.

We made it through that night unharmed, but the real miracle was internal.

For the first time, I understood what Scripture means when it says:

"He will cover you with His feathers, and under His wings you will find refuge."

Hope grounded me that night in a way I had never experienced before. It reminded me that God's presence doesn't always look like the absence of danger. Sometimes it looks like strength in the middle of it.

Helping Others: Hope Finds You When You Give It Away

One of the most surprising discoveries of my healing journey is that hope grows stronger when you share it. I experienced this firsthand during a volunteer session at a high school in my hometown.

I sat in a circle with students who were navigating bullying, discrimination, broken homes, and fear. Their stories echoed pieces of my own childhood. One boy said, "God doesn't love everyone. He plays favorites." His words hit me like a punch to the chest because I used to believe the same thing.

Something in me opened. I leaned in and told him gently, "I've felt that too. But I realized later I wasn't seeing the whole story."

In that moment, I wasn't giving advice. I was giving companionship. And companionship is often the doorway to hope.

Helping others didn't just give them hope.

It gave me mine back.

Hope Through Faith

Faith has always been the thread that ties my story together. Not because everything suddenly became easy once I trusted God, but because trusting God gave purpose to my pain and direction to my healing.

Faith taught me that hope isn't optimism.

- Hope isn't denial.
- Hope isn't pretending everything is fine.
- Hope is believing that God can redeem what seemed irredeemable.
- Hope is trusting that healing is possible even when it is slow.
- Hope is knowing you're held even when you feel broken.

My relationship with God deepened when I realized He wasn't watching from afar. He was walking beside me through every layer of healing. Through every panic attack, every relapse into shame, every flashback, every sleepless night, every setback, every triumph.

Hope grew through Scripture that met me exactly where I was:

- "I am with you always."

- "Do not fear, for I am with you."

- "He gives strength to the weary."

Hope didn't change my past.

But it transformed my relationship to it.

What Hope Actually Does

Here is one of the few lists that belongs in this chapter.

It is simple, but it captures what hope does in a survivor's life.

Hope Gives You...

- A reason to try again tomorrow

- Courage to face wounds instead of avoid them

- Compassion for yourself during setbacks

- Strength to seek support instead of hiding

- Vision for a future that is not defined by your past

- Hope is fuel.

- Hope is oxygen.

- Hope is the whisper that says, "Keep going."

Moving From Surviving to Thriving

For years, I lived in survival mode. It was the only way I knew how to function. But healing showed me that surviving is not the same as living. Surviving is about getting through. Thriving is about growing.

The shift from surviving to thriving didn't happen overnight. It happened in small, sacred steps, moments where I chose faith over fear, connection over isolation, presence over numbness, truth over shame.

- Thriving doesn't mean the trauma is gone.

- It means the trauma no longer makes your decisions for you.

- Thriving means you can feel joy without fear.

- It means you can love without bracing.

- It means you can rest without guilt.

- It means you can trust again, carefully, slowly, but truly.

Thriving means you can look at your story and see not just the wounds, but the healing woven through them.

A Short List for Those Beginning to Hope Again

Three Truths That Help Hope Take Root

1. You are not too broken for healing.

2. Healing doesn't erase your past, it transforms its power.

3. Hope grows slowly, but it grows steadily once planted.

If you can believe those three truths even a little, hope has already begun its work.

Closing Reflection

Hope didn't come to me in a dramatic moment. It came through ordinary days, quiet prayers, unexpected lifelines, and small acts of bravery I didn't recognize as bravery at the time. It came through the people God placed in my life, the opportunities I never saw coming, and the grace that met me exactly where I was.

Hope changes everything.

Not because it removes pain, but because it reveals purpose.

Not because it makes life easier, but because it makes life meaningful.

Not because it fixes the past, but because it frees the future.

Your story is not defined by what happened to you.

It is defined by what can happen next.

And no matter where you are in your journey, hope is already reaching for you.

You are not beyond healing.

You are not beyond redemption.

You are not too far gone.

Hope changes everything, and your story is still being written.

EPILOGUE

Dear Younger Me

There are moments in healing when the past stops feeling like a shadow and starts feeling like a story, one you can finally look at without collapsing under its weight. When I reached that place, something unexpected happened: I found myself thinking of the boy I used to be. The frightened kid who lived under the constant threat of emotional storms he couldn't predict and couldn't escape. The child who hid more than he played, who worried more than he laughed, who learned early how to brace for impact.

And one day, without planning it, I felt an overwhelming desire to talk to him.

This epilogue is that conversation. It is both a letter and a prayer, an embrace across time. It is what I wish someone had said to me when I was too young to understand the wounds I carried. Maybe these words will speak to the part of you that has its own younger version, waiting to hear something similar.

To the Boy I Once Was

Dear Younger Me,

If I could crawl back through the years and sit beside you on those nights when fear wrapped around you like a second skin, I would. If I could lie down on the floor next to you when you hid under your bed, wondering if tonight would be the night the yelling turned into something worse, I would. If I could speak into your confusion and loneliness, I would do it without hesitation.

You have carried so much by yourself.

More than any child should ever carry.

You think you're alone because you don't see anyone stepping in to help. You think you're invisible because the people who should have protected you didn't. You think you're unimportant because your needs were ignored, dismissed, or minimized. But none of this is true.

You are not invisible.

You are not unimportant.

You are not alone.

I know it feels that way.

But I promise you, your story isn't over yet.

And one day, you will understand that God never abandoned you, not for a moment. He was there in every tear you hid, every moment your heart raced, every night you prayed for peace you didn't receive. His presence wasn't absent just because the pain was present. He carried you through things you should never have had to experience.

One day, you'll look back and see that He was there even in the moments that broke you.

You Are Not What Happened to You

Little one, you have learned to blame yourself for things that were never your fault. You think the yelling means you did something wrong. You think the anger means you weren't good enough. You think the chaos means you caused it. You think the disappointment in others' eyes means you failed them.

Let me say this clearly:

None of it was your fault.

Not a single thing.

You were a child living in an environment that demanded the strength of a grown man.

And somehow, you survived.

You think your sensitivity is a weakness. You believe your compassion makes you easy to hurt. You think your alertness is a flaw. But these are not weaknesses. These are survival instincts. They are evidence of how hard you tried to adapt to a world that didn't feel safe.

Your body learned to protect you.

Your heart learned to anticipate danger.

Your mind learned to create safety where none existed.

These skills kept you alive.

But one day, those same skills will become the things that weigh you down. You'll think they are defects. You'll wonder why you can't just relax like everyone else. You'll wonder why you jump at loud noises, why conflict makes you freeze, why closeness scares you, and why you always want to please everyone around you.

When that day comes, I want you to remember this:

The reactions you hate are the very ones that saved you.

And once you understand that, you will start to treat yourself with the compassion you needed all along.

You Will Grow Into Someone You Can Be Proud Of

I know it's hard to believe right now, but the boy who feels small, scared, and insignificant will grow into someone strong, compassionate, and full of purpose. You will accomplish things that will surprise even you.

One day, you will walk the halls of Harvard, even though you were once convinced you weren't smart enough. One day, you will lead teams and build things and help people, even though you were once convinced you had nothing to offer. One day, you will become a father who is present, gentle, and loving, even though you rarely saw that kind of fatherhood modeled.

You think you're weak because you cry easily.

You think you're weak because your body trembles when voices rise.

You think you're weak because you can't stop trying to make everyone happy.

But you are not weak.

You are one of the strongest people I know.

Strength isn't the absence of fear.

Strength is surviving in its presence.

And you have done that every day of your young life.

You Will Be Loved Without Conditions

Love is confusing for you right now. You see it mixed with fear, tangled with anger, and wrapped in inconsistency. You think love means keeping people happy at any cost. You think love means anticipating moods, fixing problems, absorbing disappointment, or staying silent to avoid conflict.

But real love doesn't work like that.
- Real love doesn't scare you.

- Real love doesn't punish you.

- Real love doesn't make you smaller so someone else can feel bigger.

- Real love doesn't disappear when you make mistakes.

One day, you will meet people who love you in ways that feel foreign at first. They won't yell. They won't belittle. They won't withdraw affection as punishment. They won't make you responsible for their emotions.

At first, you won't trust it.

You will wait for it to crumble like everything else did.

But slowly, cautiously, you will let yourself believe it is real.

You will have a wife who sees the parts of you that still tremble and loves you even more because of them. She will stand by you as you unravel old wounds and rebuild new patterns. She will not leave when you shut down. She will stay. She will understand. She will help you breathe.

You will have children who look at you as if you hung the moon. Their trust will heal places in you that never received trust in return. Their innocence will soften the corners of your heart. Their love will call you into a better version of yourself.

Love will not destroy you.

Love will redeem you.

Your Wounds Will Become Your Testimony

Right now, your pain feels pointless. It feels cruel, random, unfair. And it is unfair. What you're living through should never happen to a child. But one day, the experiences that nearly crushed you will become the very experiences that allow you to help others.

You will sit across from teenagers who feel lost, abandoned, scared, confused, and you will understand them in a way no textbook ever could. You will mentor people who think God plays favorites, and you will tell them He doesn't. You will share parts of your story with adults who have never named their own wounds, and they will cry because your honesty will give them courage.

You will walk into rooms and instantly recognize wounded souls because you were one.

You will speak hope into people who believe they're beyond reach because you once believed that too.

You will build things, programs, and communities that remind people they are not alone.

Your pain will not be wasted.

It will become purpose.

Forgiveness Will Set You Free

There will come a day when you have to confront what happened. Not with anger, though anger will come. Not with denial, though denial will try to protect you. Not with bitterness, even though bitterness will feel justified.

You will confront your past with grief first. Then compassion. Then truth.

And eventually, forgiveness.

Forgiveness doesn't mean what happened was okay.

Forgiveness doesn't mean the people who hurt you were right.

Forgiveness doesn't mean you forget.

Forgiveness means the pain no longer controls you.

It means the story is yours to tell, not something that holds you captive.

It means you release the weight you've been carrying so you can rise into the person you were meant to become.

Forgiveness is freedom.

And you deserve to be free.

You Will Not Walk Alone

Little one, I need you to hear this: God has never left you. Even when you felt abandoned, He was there. Even when you cried alone, He collected every tear. Even when you felt unloved, He held you close. Even when you didn't believe in Him, He believed in you.

You will find healing through therapy. Through friendships. Through love. Through vulnerability. Through honesty. Through community. Through your faith. Through the wisdom of people sent to support you.

But beneath all those lifelines, God will be the anchor.

- *He will guide you.*
- *He will comfort you.*
- *He will strengthen you.*
- *He will carry you.*
- *He will redeem every part of your story.*

"He heals the brokenhearted and binds up their wounds" will stop being a verse you read and become a reality you live.

A Final Word to the Boy Inside Me

You survived what could have destroyed you.

You endured what no child should ever endure.

And you kept going, even on days when you had no reason to believe things would get better.

Everything I am today began with your courage.

The man I became is because the boy I was refused to give up.

If I could hold your face in my hands, look into your eyes, and speak one final truth, it would be this:

You are loved.

You are worthy.

You are chosen.

You are stronger than you know.

And your story, our story, will help others heal.

Thank you for surviving so I could live.

Thank you for enduring so I could grow.

Thank you for holding on so I could finally let go.

Everything is going to be okay.

Everything is going to change.

And you, little one, will become someone extraordinary.

With all the love in the world,

Your Older Self

Bibliography

Felitti, V., & Anda, R. The ACE Study, CDC–Kaiser Permanente (1998).

Burke Harris, Nadine. *The Deepest Well* (2018).

Van der Kolk, Bessel. *The Body Keeps the Score* (2014).

Perry, Bruce & Winfrey, Oprah. *What Happened to You?* (2021).

Courtois, Christine. *It's Not You, It's What Happened to You* (2009).

Walker, Pete. *Complex PTSD: From Surviving to Thriving* (2013).

Fisher, Janina. *Healing the Fragmented Selves of Trauma Survivors* (2017).

U.S. Department of Health & Human Services. *Child Maltreatment* Annual Report (latest).

Center on the Developing Child, Harvard University. Toxic Stress Framework.

Scan the QR Code to Access:

- Printable grounding exercises
- "What to Say" conversation scripts
- A list of trauma-informed therapists
- Warning signs in children
- Emergency hotline info
- John's recommended reading list

Resources for Hope, Healing, and Next Steps

Healing from Complex PTSD isn't a straight path — it's a lifelong partnership between you, your support system, and God's grace.

This section is designed to give you practical tools, questions, and resources so that your healing journey continues long after this book ends.

1. Self-Assessment: "Do I Have C-PTSD?"

This is **not** a diagnostic test, but it can help you recognize patterns common to survivors of chronic trauma.

Check any statements that resonate deeply:

Emotional & Psychological

- I often feel "on edge," anxious, or hyperaware.

- My emotions shift quickly and feel out of proportion.

- I have sudden floods of sadness, fear, or shame without a clear trigger.

- I'm highly self-critical or carry a deep sense of inadequacy.

- I struggle with trust — even with safe people.

- I feel detached or disconnected from myself or others.

Physical

- I experience chronic pain, headaches, digestive problems, or insomnia.
- My body often feels tense.
- Loud noises, sudden movements, or raised voices trigger a strong physical response.

Behavioral

- I withdraw when overwhelmed.
- I change who I am depending on who I'm with.
- I use substances, food, work, or busyness to cope with emotions.
- I avoid conflict at all costs.
- I have perfectionistic tendencies rooted in fear.

Relational

- I fear abandonment or rejection.
- I become anxious when someone is upset with me.
- I take responsibility for other people's feelings.

Background

- I experienced ongoing stress, chaos, fear, or abuse in childhood.
- Someone who was supposed to protect me caused harm.

If you checked **8 or more**, C-PTSD may be worth exploring with a trauma-informed professional.

2. Day One Healing Action Plan

When you're newly aware of trauma, it's hard to know where to start.

Here's a simple five-step plan you can begin today:

1. Name One Truth

Say aloud or write:

"I am injured, not broken. Healing is possible for me."

2. Create One Safe Space

A chair.

A corner.

A prayer spot.

A journal.

Your car.

Anywhere your nervous system can breathe.

3. Tell One Safe Person

You don't need to tell your whole story.

Just say:

"I'm struggling with things from my past, and I want to start healing."

4. Make One Appointment

A trauma-informed therapist, counselor, or pastor.

Commit to the first step — not the whole staircase.

5. Choose One Daily Regulation Practice

Pick one:

- Deep breathing
- Grounding (5–4–3–2–1)
- Brief prayer or meditation
- Gentle stretching

- Short walk

- Gratitude reflection

Consistency beats intensity.

3. Finding a Trauma-Informed Therapist

A good therapist doesn't fix you — they guide you toward your own strength.

What to Look For

- Experience with **Complex PTSD** or chronic childhood trauma

- A calm, compassionate style

- Willingness to explore your story, not just your symptoms

- No rush to diagnose without context

- Respect for your faith and values

- Training in one or more of the following:

Recommended Trauma Therapies

EMDR (Eye Movement Desensitization and Reprocessing)

One of the most effective treatments for trauma.

Somatic Experiencing / Body-Based Therapies

Teaches the body how to calm itself and release stored tension.

IFS (Internal Family Systems)

Helps heal the "younger parts" of yourself still carrying pain.

Trauma-Focused Cognitive Behavioral Therapy

Useful for identifying patterns and reframing beliefs.

Attachment-Based Therapy

Addresses relational wounds.

Faith-Based Counseling

Integrates spirituality into the healing process.

If a therapist dismisses your trauma or minimizes your experience, it's okay — even necessary — to find someone who sees you fully.

4. Warning Signs in Children

If you're a parent, teacher, or caring adult, here are signs that a child may be struggling with trauma:

Emotional
- Sudden anger or withdrawal
- Excessive fearfulness
- Difficulty regulating emotions

Behavioral
- Flinching at loud sounds
- Perfectionism
- Extreme people-pleasing
- Aggression or shutdown
- Regression (bedwetting, clinginess)

Physical
- Frequent stomachaches or headaches
- Sleep disturbances
- Flinching

Relational
- Difficulty forming friendships
- Distrust of adults
- Overly mature or overly clingy behavior

What Helps
- Predictability

- Calm tone

- Clear boundaries

- Gentle reassurance

- One consistent, safe adult

- Positive attention

And most importantly:

Believe them. Every time.

5. Books & Resources for Deeper Learning

These resources have helped me personally or align closely with trauma science and healing:

C-PTSD & Trauma
- *Complex PTSD: From Surviving to Thriving* — Pete Walker

- *The Body Keeps the Score* — Dr. Bessel van der Kolk

- *It's Not You, It's What Happened to You* — Dr. Christine Courtois

- *What Happened to You?* — Bruce Perry & Oprah Winfrey

- *The Deepest Well* — Nadine Burke Harris

Faith & Healing
- *Emotionally Healthy Spirituality* — Peter Scazzero

- *Boundaries* — Cloud & Townsend

- *The Purpose Driven Life* — Rick Warren

- *Get Out of Your Head* — Jennie Allen

Addiction & Recovery
- *The Big Book* — Alcoholics Anonymous

- *Breathing Under Water* — Richard Rohr

- Celebrate Recovery materials

For Men
- *Wild at Heart* — John Eldredge
- *Hidden Wounds* — Men's trauma groups (various churches)

6. Organizations That Can Help

Trauma & Mental Health
- **NAMI (National Alliance on Mental Illness)**

nami.org
- **SAMHSA National Helpline**

1-800-662-HELP
- **National Child Traumatic Stress Network**

nctsn.org

Domestic Violence & Abuse
- **National Domestic Violence Hotline**

1-800-799-SAFE
- **RAINN (Rape, Abuse & Incest National Network)**

rainn.org

Christian Counseling & Spiritual Support
- **Focus on the Family Counselor Line**
- **Stephen Ministries**
- **Celebrate Recovery Groups**

Suicide Prevention
- **988 Suicide & Crisis Lifeline** (U.S.)

Call or text **988** anytime.

If you are ever in immediate danger, call emergency services right away.

7. Questions to Bring to Your Provider

Print or save these questions for appointments:

1. "How does trauma influence the symptoms I'm experiencing?"

2. "Do you differentiate between PTSD and C-PTSD?"

3. "Do you offer trauma-informed therapy or refer to someone who does?"

4. "How can we incorporate my faith into my healing process?"

5. "What are healthy ways I can regulate my nervous system day-to-day?"

6. "Do you have experience treating clients with childhood trauma histories?"

7. "How will we measure progress together?"

You're not interviewing to impress them.

You're interviewing for your healing.

8. Scriptures for Healing & Hope

Here are verses to anchor your spirit as you heal:

- **Psalm 34:18** — *"The Lord is near to the brokenhearted..."*
- **Isaiah 41:10** — *"So do not fear, for I am with you..."*
- **Psalm 91:4** — *"He will cover you with his feathers, and under his wings you will find refuge."*
- **Romans 8:28** — *"God works all things for good..."*
- **2 Corinthians 12:9** — *"My grace is sufficient for you..."*
- **Psalm 46:1** — *"God is our refuge and strength..."*
- **John 8:32** — *"Then you will know the truth, and the truth will set you free."*

These verses are not bandages.

They are reminders that you are held, known, and never alone.

Closing Note

If you're reading these pages, it means you're choosing healing.

You're choosing truth.

You're choosing courage.

You're choosing hope.

And hope — as this entire book has shown — truly changes everything.

The key clinical / research claims referenced

(1) ACE Study (Adverse Childhood Experiences)

Felitti & Anda, CDC-Kaiser ACE Study (1998) — the foundational research.

(2) Lifespan reduction of up to 20 years

Nadine Burke Harris — *The Deepest Well* (2018)

(3) Trauma mimics ADHD, bipolar, anxiety, depression

Bessel van der Kolk — *The Body Keeps the Score*

(4) Hypervigilance and brain physiology

Bruce Perry — *What Happened to You?*

(5) Toxic stress reshaping the developing brain

Center on the Developing Child — Harvard University (Toxic Stress Framework)

(6) 7.2 million children reported to CPS yearly

U.S. Department of Health & Human Services — Child Maltreatment Annual Report (latest year)

(7) 91% of child abuse cases involve parents

U.S. DHHS, National Child Abuse and Neglect Data System (NCANDS)

(8) Trauma's impact on the nervous system (freeze, shut down, emotional flashbacks)

Pete Walker — *Complex PTSD: From Surviving to Thriving*

(9) 1 in 4 children experience abuse or neglect

Child Abuse Prevention Network — Facts and Statistics

(10) Prevalence of adverse childhood experiences among U.S. adults

Centers for Disease Control and Prevention — Morbidity and Mortality Weekly Report 72, no. 26 (2023)

MORE FROM JOHN

JohnPBoyle.com

www.ingramcontent.com/pod-product-compliance
Lightning Source LLC
Chambersburg PA
CBHW031150130726
47988CB00006B/2624